THREE PLAYS BY
DAVID GARRICK

DAVID GARRICK
From the portrait by Robert Edge Pine in the Henry E. Huntington
Library.

THREE PLAYS BY
DAVID GARRICK

*Printed from hitherto unpublished
mss. with introductions and notes by*

ELIZABETH P. STEIN, *Ph.D.*

Benjamin Blom
New York

First published 1926 by
Wm. Edwin Rudge
Reissued 1967 by
Benjamin Blom, Inc. New York 10452
Library of Congress Cat. Card No. 67-23858

PRINTED IN THE U.S.A.

PREFACE

IN the course of some researches for a study of David Garrick, I had the good fortune to come upon several unpublished Garrick manuscripts and a portrait of this celebrated player. Of these, the manuscripts included in this book are the three hitherto unpublished Garrick plays: (1) *Harlequin's Invasion*, 1759, the original of which is in the Barton-Ticknor Collection of the Boston Public Library; (2) *The Jubilee*, 1769; and (3) *The Meeting of the Company or Bayes's Art of Acting*, 1774; the originals of which form part of the Henry E. Huntington Library.

Except for the fact that in 1858 the manuscript, *Harlequin's Invasion*, was the property of Mr. Thomas Barton of New York City, the history of this manuscript is unknown. The Huntington manuscripts, however, were originally in the collection of Garrick's illustrious successor, John Philip Kemble, who collected as many English plays as he was able to lay his hands on. This collection, which includes some nine thousand plays, some of them very choice and rare editions, furnishes considerable information regarding the rise and development of the English drama. In 1820, Kemble sold his collection to William George Spencer Cavendish, Sixth Duke of Devonshire, who paid for this invaluable material two thousand pounds. While in the Duke's hands, it was considerably enlarged and later became known as the Kemble-Devonshire Collection.[1]

In January, 1914, this collection passed into the hands of the famous American collector, Mr. Henry Edwards Huntington, who has kindly permitted me to publish from it the two long-lost Garrick plays, *The Jubilee* and *The Meeting of the Company or Bayes's Art of Acting*. A somewhat more extended discussion of these three Garrick plays than is appropriate to the individual introductions of this book will be included in my forthcoming volume, *David Garrick, Dramatist*.

The original portrait, a reproduction of which serves as the frontispiece to the present volume, adorned, at the time I did my research, one of the walls of the catalogue room of Mr. Huntington's library in New York City. As far as can be ascertained, this portrait, which was painted by Robert Edge Pine, to whom Garrick sat for several portraits, has never before been published. The date of this likeness is unknown, but if one may judge from the plumpness of both face and form, it shows Garrick rather late in life. The actor is here represented in the rôle of private gentleman.

I desire to avail myself of this opportunity to acknowledge my indebtedness to the various persons who have so kindly aided me in the production of this book.

To Mr. Henry Edwards Huntington, whose generous permission has made possible the publication of this hitherto unpublished Garrick material, I wish to express my grateful appreciation.

To my friend and teacher, Professor Arthur Huntington

---

[1] This Collection contains fifty-seven Shakespearean quartos and four folios.

Nason of New York University, are due my sincere thanks for the many valuable suggestions he has given me in the preparation of this volume.

To Dr. George Watson Cole, former Librarian of the Henry E. Huntington Library, who was instrumental in obtaining for me Mr. Huntington's consent to the publication of this unpublished Garrick material, I am especially indebted. To him and also to the staff, I wish to express my thanks for the many enjoyable hours I spent in the Huntington Library.

My thanks are also due to Mr. William Seymour (for twenty years General Stage Director of the Charles Frohman Company) for his interpretation of the various stage directions in the play *Harlequin's Invasion*. Mr. Seymour's explanations will be found in the notes following the text of this play.

To Mr. Otto Fleischner, former Director of the Boston Public Library, who, when that library closed its doors to the general public during the prevalency of the influenza (September, 1918), permitted me to continue my research there unmolested; to Mr. Charles F. D. Belden, the present Director of the Boston Public Library; to Mr. Samuel Chevalier and Miss M. Louise Cassidy, of the general staff of the Boston Public Library; to Mrs. Lillian A. Hall, assistant in the Theatre Collection of the Harvard University Library; and to the Massachusetts Historical Society, I wish to express my appreciation for their kind co-operation.

E. P. S.

New York City,
September 14, 1925.

TABLE OF CONTENTS

LIST OF ILLUSTRATIONS

HARLEQUIN'S INVASION

with Transparency's etc.

INTRODUCTION

I N THE PROLOGUE, which Garrick spoke at the
opening of the Drury Lane Theatre on September 8,
1750, he declared his theatre sacred to Shakespeare.
Moreover, he threatened to abandon the better plays and
feed the public on spectacular entertainments if he found
that Harlequin was preferred to his Hamlet and Lear.

At Covent Garden, John Rich, the manager of that
theatre, was achieving phenomenal success with his panto-
mimes. So excellent and so brilliantly original were his
pantomimic representations that, as time went on, his har-
lequinades grew more popular than Garrick's finest Shakespearean performances, with the result that there was a
falling off of receipts at the Drury Lane Theatre. Garrick
sought to remedy this evil, and for the Christmas holidays
of 1750, he presented the Town with an entertainment
called *Queen Mab,* in which Woodward, as Harlequin,
proved himself a worthy rival of the celebrated Lun, as
Rich was known on the stage. The success of this pantomime was so great that "Rich began to tremble on his
throne." From that day forward pantomime, spectacle, and
musical entertainments found a regular place upon the
program of the Drury Lane Theatre.

On December 31, 1759,[1] Garrick produced his panto-

---

[1] Genest, *English Stage,* 1832, IV, 580.

mime, *Harlequin's Invasion*, the text of which follows these prefatory remarks. Contrary to all pantomimic rules, the characters in this harlequinade speak. In the prologue to a later presentation of this play, probably sometime immediately after the death of Rich, which occurred in November, 1761, Garrick explained the reason for introducing speaking characters into his pantomime and, at the same time, paid high tribute to the superiority of Lun's art.

> But why a speaking Harlequin?—'tis wrong,
> The wits will say, to give the fool a tongue:
> When Lun appear'd with matchless art and whim,
> He gave the pow'r of speech to ev'ry limb;
> Tho' mask'd and mute, convey'd his quick intent,
> And told in frolic gestures all he meant.
> But now the motley coat, and sword of wood,
> Requires a tongue to make them understood.[2]

The plot of Garrick's play, which is built upon the pantomime presented at Goodman's Fields Theatre, March 2, 1741,[3] called *Harlequin Student, or the Fall of Pantomime with the Restoration of the Drama*, deals with Harlequin's invasion of Shakespeare's territory, Parnassus, his expulsion therefrom, and finally the triumph of poetry and drama over pantomime. Closely woven into this plot is the story of Tailor Joe Snip, who, at the instigation of his shrewish wife, sets out, clad in armor and armed with sword, in quest of Harlequin's head; the loss and regaining of his own; Dolly Snip's love-affair with Harlequin; her taking on airs in the expectation of becoming a fine lady; her quarrel with her plebeian suitor; the latter's engage-

---

[2] Garrick, *Poetical Works*, 1785, I, 158.

[3] Genest, III, 641.

[4]

ment to Dolly's cousin; and finally the home-coming of the knight-errant, Tailor Snip. All these episodes are well worked out. The humor throughout the play is fairly good.

Harlequin's Invasion was a successful piece. It had occasional revivals, the latest of which, recorded by Genest, took place on April 8, 1820,[4] after which date it was acted nineteen times. During this revival the pantomime was called *Shakespeare versus Harlequin.* Some of Garrick's text in this version was omitted and a good deal of new material inserted; but these changes did not improve the play.

The original cast of *Harlequin's Invasion* included the following players: Thomas King, who was the Harlequin of the play; Richard Yates, who took the part of Joe Snip; John Moody, who played Simon, the Clown; Blakes, who acted Gasconade, the Frenchman; Bransby, who personated Barnaby Bounce; and Miss Pope, who acted Dolly Snip in admirable style.

HARLEQUIN'S INVASION

with Transparency's etc.

Act 1st

Scene 1st   Charing Cross.   (2d Grove)

Enter Bog. Taffy, Forge with a Paper Crib &c huzzaing

Forge.

Here, here it is! Huzza Boys — here it is, my Jolly
Hearts! — this will be the making of us all, Huzza!

Taffy.

Vat you got neiper Forge?

{(2)
{Bounce
{a Stick

Forge.

Damn me if I know what it is; but it will be the
making of us all! Here, read it, read it Taffy.
It will be the making of us all!

{(3)
{Gasconade

Taffy.

I will put on my best Eyes. neipor Forge, and do your
likings.

Bog.

Hold your hand my dear, for tho' you read it very
well, I don't understand a word you say.

{(4)
{Mercury
{followers
{& Chorus.

Taffy.

Read it yourself.

Bog.

Faith I can't Honey, I write very well; but I forgot
my Reading long ago (_Enter Bounce Pd_

Garrick's _Harlequin's Invasion_, I, i. From the MS. in the Barton-
Ticknor Collection of the Boston Public Library.

ACT I

SCENE I. *Charing Cross* (2d *Grove*)

Enter BOG. TAFFY, FORGE *with a Paper* CRIB ETC. *huzzaing.*

FORGE: Here, here it is! Huzza Boys—here it is, my Jolly Hearts!—this will be the making of us all, Huzza!

[(2) BOUNCE *a Stick*]

TAFFY: Vat you got Neipor Forge?

FORGE: Damn me if I know what it is; but it will be the making of us all! Here, read it, read it Taffy. It will be the making of us all! [(3) GASCONADE]

TAFFY: I will put on my best Eyes, Neipor Forge, and do your likings.

BOG: Hold your hand my dear, for tho' you read it very well, I don't understand a word you say.

[(4) MERCURY, *followers &* CHORUS]

TAFFY: Read it yourself.

BOG: Faith I can't Honey, I write very well; but I forgot my Reading long ago. [*Enter* BOUNCE *Pd.*]

BOUNCE: Where is it? where is it? Zounds! let me see it.

TAFFY: Here it is, Neipor Pounce, the Corporal.

BOUNCE: What do you give it me for? You know I can't Read. I can swear, I can fight, I can drink, I can Wench. I can——

TAFFY: You can Teeve and Steal too.

BOUNCE: Zounds I can do any thing but Read; and as for that why I am a Soldier, and above it.

[11]

TAFFY: Tis apove you, you mean, foolish Man.

> [*Enter* GASCONADE *O P.*]

GASCON: Pourquoy faites vous tant de bruit—Vat is all dis Noise?

BOUNCE: For my pleasure: I love Noise, and hate the French, And my Name is Barnaby Bounce.

GASCON: Your Name is Barnaby Villaine, Poltroon; and Begar, if you are not a little more Poli, Je vous Donnerai le Coup de pied! I vil kick a you behind.

BOUNCE: Well, well; I believe you dare fight; So I won't quarrel with you. Here's my Hand, I'm your Friend.

GASCON: De tout Mon Coeur! Look you, Sir. I dare Fight de Devil. but I had much rather be friend with de Devil, So Sir; I am your tres humble Serviteur. Mais Allons. Vat Papier is dat?

BOUNCE: Give it me—Give it me—Here you dismal [*to* CRIB]. You can Read I know; He's a special Scholar. He was formerly a Parish Clerk, and was turn'd out of his office, for robbing the Poors Box.

CRIB: And so I was indeed.

> [*Sound & Shout.*]

BOUNCE: Stand clear! Stand clear! Here comes the Herald Himself. Huzza.

> [(5) SNIP, M^{RS}. SNIP, *Measures & Shears*]

ALL: Huzza! Huzza—[*Flourish*]

Enter 2 Heralds, Staves [*P S*], 2 Trumpets, Drum & Fife, Mercury, 2 Heralds, Staves, All the Chorus.

Roar Trumpet, Squeak Fife, blow Horn & beat Drum.

> [*Flourish*]

[12]

To Dramatica's Realm, from Apollo I come.
Whereas it is fear'd a French trick may be play'd ye
Be it known Monsr Harlequin, means to invade ye.
And hither transporting his Legions, He floats
On an Ocean of Canvass in Flat bottom Boats:
With Fairies, Hags, Genii, Hobgoblins all shocking
And many a Devil in flame colour'd Stocking
Let the light Troops of Comedy March to attack him,
And Tragedy whet all her Daggers to Hack Him.
Let all hands, and hearts, do their utmost Endeavour;
Sound Trumpet, beat Drum, King Shakespeare forever.

[Flourish & Shout]

Air

> To arms you brave Mortals to arms,
> The Road to Renown is before you.
> The Name of King Shakespear has Charms,
> To rouze you to Actions of Glory.

2

> Away, ye brave Mortals away,
> 'Tis nature calls on you to save her,
> What Man, but wou'd nature obey
> And Fight for her Shakespear forever.

[Shout Flourish & Exeunt O P]

SCENE II. *Plain Chamber (Bor. and W s. Bell)*

Enter JOE SNIP & WIFE *pushing him on P. S.*

WIFE: Get along you cowardly Rascal, and make your Fortune at once. Follow 'em, follow 'em, don't you hear the Trumpet?

SNIP: Yes, and You too Wife, You are both loud enough, I am sure.

WIFE: Sirrah, Sirrah, and I'll be louder still, What have you no Manhood left? have not you Spirit enough to take Fire at the proclamation?

SNIP: You have Spirit enough Wife to take Fire at any Thing. You make a Proclamation in my Ears every Day of *my Life*. the Trumpets are a Fool to You.

WIFE: You poor, mean, low minded Fellow! Can nothing rouze you? Is all my greatness of Soul thrown away upon you? Upon a Taylor?

     [(6) SIMON, HARLEQUIN, ALL THE CHILDREN]

SNIP: I wish it had been thrown into the Sea, with all my Soul, before I had been honour'd with it.

WIFE: How villain! Do you wish *me* in the Sea?

SNIP: Yes from my Soul do I: if wishing wou'd do me any *Good*.

WIFE: Here's a wicked Wretch for you! Don't provoke me I say with your disobedience. Away with your Thread Lists and your Measures! Put on a Sword and bring me this Frenchman's Head on the point of it. and at once make me a Lady and Yourself a Lord.

SNIP: Make you a Widow, and myself a Fool you mean. I bring you his Head upon the point of a Sword. Bring you a Flea's Head upon the point of a Needle.

WIFE: Sirrah! Sirrah, don't provoke me, I say.

SNIP: You shall never provoke me to Fight Wife:—When can I find a Heart to cut off Heads; Your Tongue must be a little quieter than it is, I can assure you that.

WIFE: Did you ever hear such a wicked Wretch. Such an Ungrateful Wretch? have I not refused the best Men, and

[14]

the best Matches for your Sake. Had I not been bewitch'd by your person, and deluded by your Tongue, I might have held up my Head with the proudest She in the parish.

SNIP: I have not held up mine, I'm sure, since you did me the favour, Heigh, ho!

WIFE: Don't stand sighing and Sniv'ling here; but rouze your Manhood. Clap a Sword by your Side and March.

SNIP: Yes, I'll march up to my Shop-board, and finish the Work I'm about. [x to P S]. Here's my two Edged Sword [takes out his Shears] No Taylor in Christendom can fight a Piece of Broad Cloth better than I can. I'll say that for myself.

WIFE: You say for yourself, you poor, mean, Beggarly, Cowardly Fellow You! Don't put me in a passion! I hate to be Quarrelsome: But you will force me to break thro' the meakness of my Spirit, and do something. I'll tell you what Joe; if you won't Exert yourself for my sake, I'll no longer be Virtuous for yours—I have my Revenge in my own Hands. and so fetch me this Outlandish Mans Head, or, take care of your own, I say—A word to the wise, take care of your own. [Exit O P.]

SNIP: Aye, there she has me; She knows how Delicate I am about my Honour; And she always attacks me in that tender point.—I must do my best to please her—I must either make a Fool of myself, or, she'll make something worse of me.

Devils we say, and justly too are Wives
And all do know,
As well as Joe,

He needs must go
The Devil drives.   *[Exit P S.]*

SCENE III. *Barn to change to Trees. And a Cave behind Stump of a Tree to change to Armour.* [2. *En. O P.*]
Harleq^n: Discov'^{d}: asleep before the Barn.

                [Enter SIMON O P. 1st Ent.]

SIMON: Ha! ha! ha! what a plague is the matter with all my Neighbours? the Murrain has seiz'd 'em I believe, they will have it, that there is some strange Creature got into the Parish, the Women are all agog to see it. the Children are frighted out of their Wits. Our Parson shakes his Head and the Squire and his Dogs are all in high Hunt after it, His Worship, our Justice; and Master Cramp the Lawyer, call'd to Me at the end of the Lane; Simon, Simon, said they what strange Creature is that in our Parish; and please your Worship says Me, I. I don't think we want strange Creatures in our Parish and so I whistled away, and left it with them. But I can't see nothing, not I—If I do chance to light on 'em, I shall make bold to tickle 'em a little with the Prongs of my Fork, Ha! ha! ha! [*Going, he sees* HARLEQUIN.] So! So! so, talk of the Devil and heres one of his Imps; why sure this can't be a living Creature—Ecod but it is—'Tis either Drunk, or asleep, or both, shall I take it dead or alive, has it nothing about it to do Mischief; I'll e'en put the Fork into it, and make all sure at once. [*touches* HARL: *who tumbles.*] Ha! ha! ha! I have set 'en a Dancing already. Hollo!

HARLEQ: Hollo! [*Sits up and rubs his Eyes.*]

SIMON: Who are you? whence came you?

HARLEQ: I am Nobody, and came from nowhere.[*Rising*]

[16]

SIMON: Where are you going then?

HARLEQ: To my own Parish. Your Ta. [*going*]

SIMON: Hold! hold Mr. Nobody, hold, hold a Bit.—As you came from no-where, and are going to the same Place, it can be no great damage to stop you a Little——

[*holds his Fork at him.*]

HARLEQ: Pray don't hurt me, Merciful Sir! I am a very harmless Creature: I have been taking a Nap here, and am not quite awake.

SIMON: Whence came you?

HARLEQ: There! [*looking up*]

SIMON: There! what as far as I can see?

HARLEQ: Farther. There!

SIMON: Where.

HARLEQ: There. [*Strikes his Hand & catches the Fork.*]

SIMON: Give me my Fork.

HARLEQ: Take it then. [*Pointing it at him.*]

SIMON: Pray don't hurt me, merciful Sir! I am but a poor harmless Creature.

HARLEQ: Ha! ha! ha! shall we be friends

SIMON: Why shall we? Eh?

HARLEQ: Ouy.

SIMON: Ouy! whats that?

HARLEQ: Yes.

SIMON: Well then, We; with all my Heart.

HARLEQ: Done. [*holds out his Hand.*]

[17]

SIMON: Done—[*holds out his*]

HARLEQ: And done. [*Strikes him with his Sword*]

SIMON: Is that the way you shew your Friendship

HARLEQ: Friend Simon—take your Fork.

[(7) SNIP *in Armour*]

SIMON: Will you give it Me?

HARLEQ: Here, take it. [*Sinks it*]

SIMON: Pray Friend, what's your Name.

HARLEQ: Whirligig.

SIMON: Whirligig, and pray Friend Whirligig; what Profession are you of?

HARLEQ: A Fly Catcher — I was formerly altogether among the Stars—I plied as a Ticket Porter in the Milky Way, and carried the Howdyes from one Planet to another; but finding that too fatiguing I got into the Service of the Rainbow, and now I wear his Livery, don't you think I Fib now Friend Simon?

SIMON: Yea, in troth do I—friend Whirligig, He! he! he!

HARLEQ: I'll settle your faith in a moment: And shew you some of my little Family. [*Strikes the Barn*]

Tr. Bell

It turns into a Cut Wood back'd by a Cave (4 G) Several Children in Pantomime Characters come down and Dance at which SIMON appears delighted.

HAR: [*End of Dance.*] Away!—away!—Vanish.—[*Children Ext. Severally*] I'm pursued! they are at my Heels! O Friend Simon I'm undone, they'll roast me alive if they take me. [*Runs about*]

[18]

SIMON: And boil me perhaps for keeping you Company. What shall we do?

HARLEQ: Courage Simon, I'll protect thee. [*They get up into the Tree*] Friend Simon, I'll shew you some Sport: Keep in your Head; the Enemy's at Hand.

[(8) Mᴿ. BOUNCE, GASCONADE]
[*P S Enter* SNIP *loaded wᵗʰ Armour.*]

SNIP: What a dismal thing it is to live in fear of ones Wife. here am I sent, a poor harmless Taylor, shaking and trembling to kill something, who wou'd make no more of killing me, than I wou'd of stealing a Piece of Cloth; every Bush, and every blast of Wind is an Ague to me, as I came along, a Sheep did but clap his Nose, thro' a Hedge, and cry Baa, and I have been in Sweat ever since. I borrow'd this Armour of a Friend of mine, formerly of the Train Bands; But he cou'dn't tell me how to put it on—I wish I could see any of my Neighbours to shew me home again, for I have almost frighted myself blind.

HARLEQ: Neighbour Snip—Neighbour Snip.

SNIP: Eh! what's that?—I am a dead Man.

HARLEQ: Be not in Panicks—I am your friend & Neighbour, Taffy.

SNIP: Where are you Neighbour, Taffy.

HARLEQ: I am got into this Tree to hide myself from Harlequin. He is just gone by with a Sword in his Hand as long, and as broad as a Scythe, and looks as Crabbed as if he had eaten sower Pippins.

SNIP: Pray Neighbour make room for me.

HARLEQ: Here's but just Room for Neighbour Pog and I.

[19]

SNIP: What is he there, too.

HARLEQ: I don't know whether I am here, or no faith; for the Gentleman with his long Sword has frighten'd Me out of my Senses, and Remembrances too Joy.

SNIP: What must I do then, pray tell me, for I am most sadly frighted.

HARLEQ: Yes faith are you! I hear it very visibly! Go into that Cave there, and you'll be very safe; and may have very good Time to sleep yourself into your Senses again.

SNIP: Thank you, I'll take your Advice, Pray Neighbour Taffy, tell Me, when you go home, that I mayn't go alone.

HARLEQ: Dat I will neighbour Snip.

SNIP: Thank you good Neighbour [*going*] Bless me! Oh! 'tis nothing.——   [*Exit into the Cave.*]

SIMON: What is he gone, Hark ye Friend Whirligig— you ar'n't afraid of a Taylor?

HARLEQ: Silence! here are more of 'em.

                [*Enter* BOUNCE & GASCONADE *P. S*]

BOUNCE: Look about, he must be here about.

GASCON: Ne faites pas tant de Bruit; Don't a you make a noise And if we can Attrap him asleep, We will cut his Troat, and save ourselves de trouble of an Engagement.

BOUNCE: 'SBlood you are not afraid, are you? [*Softly*]
                                [(9) FORGE *Drunk*]

GASCON: Non, non, I am only prudent.

BOUNCE: You don't like to kill your Countryman, then.

GASCON: I beg your pardon: I wou'd kill anything for my Interest.

[20]

BOUNCE: You remember the Bargain? We go Snacks in the Murder.

GASCON: Ouy! Ouy!—Begar he shall cut off de Head himself And I will snack a de money. Eh! Monsuier Bounce What is de Raison your one two knees knicky knocky together, come sa?

BOUNCE: Oh! that proceeds from my Eagerness for Fighting—My Flesh quivers to be at him—Trembling is a sure Sign of Resolution.

GASCON: Upon my word den, Vous et moy, You and I have so much Resolution, as any two in all de varld.

BOUNCE: What can be the matter with me—If I should continue Sweating for a Day as I do now, I should be melted down to the Lathy consistency of Joe Snip the Taylor. [*aside.*]

HARLEQ: Who calls me?

BOUNCE: Eh! What the Devil's that?

GASCON: If you no like it, I vil go home avec a vous vid all mine heart.

HARLEQ: 'Tis only I; Joseph Snip in the Tree here.

GASCON: Vat you do dere, Eh?

HARLEQ: Hush! Hush! Harlequin is hard by.

BOTH: Where! Where?

HARLEQ: In that Cave there: I believe he is asleep.

BOUNCE: Will you go and wake him. and tell him I'm come to murder him.

GASCON: Non, non; you had much better kill Him first, and there will be no occasion to Wake him at all.

[21]

BOUNCE: We'll nap him sleeping.

GASCON: De tout Mon Coeur.—Allons!

BOUNCE: Lead the way.

GASCON: Non, indeed; Sir

BOUNCE: Go first I say!

GASCON: I am une Francoise & understand Civility, I vil not go first upon my Vard!

BOUNCE: We'll go together, give me your Hand

[Exit into Cave]

SIMON: Well, but friend Whirligig, You won't let 'em kill the poor Taylor.

HARLEQ: They'll cut off his Head only. But I'll give him a better.

BOUNCE & GASCON: *[Huzza within]*

[Enter FORGE *Drunk P S]*

What the Devil do you make such a Noise for.

[Enter BOUNCE & GASCONADE *(from Top.)]*

BOUNCE: 'Tis done! 'tis done! this is the Arm that gave the Blow. *[Gives the Head to* FORGE]*

GASCON: Vat is you say? Parblieu! I say, and I swear dis vas de Bon Sword dat dit cut off de Head.

BOUNCE: Right Frenchman, but this was the Sword that lay'd him low first.

GASCON: Vous Mentez, You lie, you Villain, how cou'd you knock him down, ven I did Cut his Troat when he vas fast asleep?

FORGE: Upon my word you are two very pretty Fellows, You have kill'd a sleeping Taylor. and are quarreling about the glory of the Victory

[22]

BOUNCE: A Taylor!

GASCON: Eh! un Tailleur!

FORGE: Really you are two very great Champions—You set out a couple of Lyon Hunters, and return a Couple of Sheep Stealers.

BOUNCE: Confusion choaks Me. [*x to OP.*]

GASCON: Begar, I am very much afraid un Rope vil Choak a Me. [*takes the Head*]

HARLEQ: Now Simon, observe the Virtue of this Shrub. Wheres my Head? Where's my Head?
[*Gets from the Tree and is chang'd to the Taylor without a head.*]

BOUNCE: Fire and Brimstone! the Devil! the Devil.
[*Exit Running O P*]

HARL: Frenchman give me my Head—Frenchman give me my Head.

GASCON: Here, begar, take a your Head, Vile I take a to my Heel.—[*Exit Running PS*]

FORGE: What a Parcel of Cowardly Dogs are my Neighbours. As if they had never seen a Taylor without a Head before—Pray my good Friend, Joseph Snip, what are your Commands?

HARLEQ: Take my Head home to my Wife; and bid her prosecute my Murderers.   [*ACT*]

FORGE: If she won't I will.—But Neighbour, if they have really murder'd you, You had better appear yourself as an Evidence, and you'll certainly hang 'em.

HARLEQ: They shall hear farther from me.

FORGE: Well, I'll be your Porter for once [*takes the*

Head] Upon my word 'tis wondrous light—Damn me if I don't think he looks better without a Head than with— We see by this of what Consequence a Head is to a Taylor
[going]

HARLEQ: Bless you good Neighbour.

FORGE: Very well, Joe, I am satisfied, no more words; pray Stay where you are: You know I hate Ceremony You have lost your Head; and may lose your way too—Pray stay where you are. *[Exit* FORGE *PS]*

[HARLEQ: *goes to the side Scene Slips his Dress & returns immediately.*]

HARL: So they are disposed off.

SIMON: What are you there friend Whirligig? Egad I thought I had lost you.

HARL: Friend Simon—I'll step into the Cave, Stitch the Taylor a new Head on, and then you shall go to Town with me; and see my Pranks there, Eh! Simon.
[Exit into the Cave.]

SIMON: Indeed I will not Master Whirligig—Egad I have had enough of your Pranks here.—No more Devils Dances for Simon, He must be old Nick himself for Sartain, and I am dealing with him. Heavens! bless me! the Thoughts of it puts me into a grevious taking: He talks of Heads as if they were so many Buttons, and cuts 'em off, and Sows 'em on, as fast,—I'll e'en steal home while I have Legs to walk upon, and my Head upon my Shoulders but is it there?—yes it is.—But I had best hold it for fear of the worst. *[Exit OP.]*

Drop: Bar Bell.
Act ends.

ACT II

SCENE *Justices Room* (2d *Groove.*)
Table 5 Chairs
The Bench of Justices all Discover'd.

[(2) CONSTABLES]

1ST JUSTICE: And now we have got him—this Harlequin —what must we do with him? What think you Brother Cramp.

2 JUSTICE: Why for my part, M^r. Chairman, I think this Harlequin comes within the Statute description of Incorrigible Rogue—He's an old Offender—and I think we have a Power to Transport Him.

1ST JUSTICE: I don't know that—We must have a care of Informations above, Master Cramp, We can't be too wary, A burnt Child you know—Call in the Head Borough.— Call in Joseph Harrow.

CLERK: Joseph Harrow, come into Court.

3D JUSTICE: What think you, Brothers of setting our hands to his Pass—and having him whip'd from Constable to Constable.

1ST JUSTICE: But where must we pass him to, M^r. Justice Spindle. This Fellow is a Vagabond; 'tis true; but he is Son to No-body—Servant to No-body,—belongs to No-body. Comes from No-where, and is going to no where. And We None of Us, No, none of us, know nothing at all about him.   [(3) HARLEQUIN & CONSTABLES]

[*Enter* CONSTABLE *P. S*]

1ST JUSTICE: Well, M^r. Constable, where is your Prisoner?

[25]

CONSTABLE: He's without, and please your Worships—I wish we were well rid of him, for under favor—I don't think he's of this world—He is certainly something as I may say of the Magical Order about him.

1ST JUSTICE: Ay, how so?

CONSTABLE: Why theres Simon Clodby of Gander Green says as how this Black a Moor Man has Cut off a Taylors Head and sow'd it on again.

2D JUSTICE: Did you ever hear the like. Why He has cut off all your Heads I think.

CONSTABLE: I think we are all in some danger; Aye and Your Worship's too. for I heard him say myself, that he cou'd cut off all your Worships Heads, and no harm done neither.

1ST JUSTICE: He'll cut off our Heads will he? We'll lay him by the Heels first. Bring him before us. He'll cut off Our Heads Quotha—And now we have got him.——

[*Enter* HARLEQUIN & CONSTABLE. *PS.*]

1ST JUSTICE: Let us first examine the Prisoner; I hear, Sir, that you have been doing a great deal of Mischief about this Country.——

HARLEQUIN: Yes, a great deal.

1ST JUSTICE: Very well, he confesses it, Set that down Clerk, & I hear that you Cut off Peoples Heads——

HARLEQ: Yes, to cure the Tooth Ach: Is your Worship troubled with it.

3D JUSTICE: You impudent Vagabond. How dare you talk to the Court so Did you tell this honest Constable here, that you wou'd Cut off our Heads.

[26]

HARLEQ: Yes, and mend 'em for nothing.

3D JUSTICE: Did you ever hear the like, let us send him to Prison directly—a little whipping will mend his manners.

ALL JUSTICES: Commit him! Commit him.

HARLEQ: Mercy, mercy, dear, good, wise, reverend, worshipful Old Gentlewoman.

ALL JUSTICES: No Mercy away with him, Away with him.
[(4) DOLLY MRS. SNIP]

HARLEQ: Nay then have at your Heads.

[*Loud Whistle & Wing Bell*]
[*Strikes the Table with his Sword. The Wigs all fly off.*

HARL: *runs off. and in their places w[h]ere the* JUSTICES *was Seated comes* 4 *Old women* (*sic*). *Soon an old woman comes forward.*]   [*Curtain Bell*]

SONG.

Old Women we are
And as wise in the Chair
As fit for the Quorum as Men
We can scold on the Bench
Or Examine a Wench
And like them can be wrong now and then.

Chorus:

For search the world thro'
And you'll find nine in Ten
Old women can do—As much as Old Men.

2d.

We can hear a sad case
With a no meaning-face

[27]

And tho' shallow yet seem to be deep
Leave all to the Clerk
For when matters grow dark
Their Worships had better go sleep.

Chorus etc.

3^d.

When our Wisdom is task'd
And hard questions are ask'd
We'll answer them best with a Snore
We can mump a Tid bit
And can Joke without Wit
And what can their Worships do more.

[*Chorus & Exit OP.*]

Cur: Bell.
Wainscot Chamb^r. (1st *Groove*)
Enter DAME SNIP & DOLLY *crying PS*

MRS. SNIP: What do you cry for Dolly, my Daughter, and want a proper Spirit, I am asham'd of your principles Dolly—What do you cry for, Child.

DOLLY: I can't help it Mama—I am asham'd to see my Papa so Blood Thirsty, and look so like a Madman as he did, with his Breast Pan and Head Pan, and a long Sword to kill that dear Sweet Charmingest of all Creatures—Harlequin.

MRS. SNIP: How dare you be so wicked to say this of a Creature that your Papa is gone to Murder—Have you no Delicacy, you disobedient slut you, My dear Joe, is coming home in Triumph to us. He has done the Business before this.——

[28]

DOLLY: But he han't nor won't, nor shan't nor can't—that I am sure of, and I hope he never will.

MRS. SNIP: Whats that you mutter, Madam, won't your Papa comprehend Harlequin.

[(5) ABRAHAM]

DOLLY: How can he, Mama, Nobody can comprehend him, He's too nimble for 'em, that's my Comfort—they hunted him last week all about the Town, and he turn (*sic*) himself into Ten thousand Shapes, first he shrunk Himself into a Dwarf. then He stretch'd himself into a Giant, then He was a Beau, then a Monkey, then a Peacock; then a Wheelbarrow, and then he made himself an Ostelige; and he walked about so stately & look'd so Grand, and when I went up to him He clap't his Wings So, [*Mimics the Ostrich*] that my very Heart leapt within me.

MRS. SNIP: More shame for you Dolly—So hold your Tongue.

DOLLY: Can't hold my Tongue, Wiser folks than you and I, Mama, prize him more than your Tragedies, or your Comedies, aye, or your Singing either; Cousin Chitterlin and I doat on him; where do you think he was Mama, when he was lost for three Days?—You'd neer Guess—I hid him in my Bed Chamber.

MRS. SNIP: In your Bed Chamber.

DOLLY: Yes, I did, and I'd hide him there again, and again and again, sure I'm old enough to know whats best for me. Lord what a Creature; He was Here & there and every where. Now He was out of the Window then a top of the House, then down in the Street, Then He run up the

Leaden Spout; Then he jump't behind the Glass—then over the Table and Chairs—then He Run under the Bed & over the Bed, & in the Bed, and there was such a Bustle, and I was in such a flutter, and at last, when He had play'd all his tricks over and over again; He whip'd across our Jenny's Broom: Gave me a hearty Kiss, whisks up the Chimney and flew into the Country where he has been ever since.

Mrs. Snip: I am shock'd at your Impudence—you'l break my Heart Dolly—You're a Jack-bite Hussey.

Dolly: A Jack-bite am I—Oh, Law!

Mrs. Snip: You are a Rebel, Madam,—you hide Rebels, and whoever hides Rebels is a Jackbite, all the World Over—Read the Newspapers.

Dolly: Bless me, I tremble every Joint of me.

Mrs. Snip: And well you may Dolly—for if your Papa can kill Harlequin, we shall not only be rich Child, but Qualitify'd.

Dolly: Ay, indeed, Qualitify'd—Shew me that and I'll send him packing, I'll warrant you

Mrs. Snip: Your Papa, will be a Barrow-Knight, a Lord at least, and they'll call me my Ladyship, and you'll be Lady Doll Snip all the World over.

Dolly: Shall I. I'd cut off his Head myself if I had him here.

Mrs. Snip: My dear Sweet Child—Now you are your Mothers own Daughter—How I love your Spirit. You have it all from my Family—You have nothing sneaking about you, like your Father

[30]

DOLLY: Pray should I let our Abraham Court me, and Slop me about any more till I hear farther from my Papa

MRS. SNIP: You may easily pick a Quarrel with him.

DOLLY: I'll frump him the next time he speaks to me [*x to PS*] I can't bear to think of a Taylor now, if I were to chuse for myself I should like a Captain.

MRS. SNIP: A Captain!

DOLLY: Yes, a Captain; they look so bold, and are so bold, and are so Grand—and when they march up to one—So— they look as if they wou'd Eat a Body. It frightens one a little. But it does ones heart Good to see 'em. I will have a Captain Mama.

MRS. SNIP: So thou shalt, I love a Soldier too; Every body Loves 'em; they have done so much, & deserve so much, that they may do what they will with us.

DOLLY: Let 'em do their worst, I defy 'em; But here comes Abram. I can't bear the sight of him.

[*Enter* ABRAM, *P. D.*]
Mistress, Master Forge, below wants to speak with you: He has News of my Master, but won't tell it to nobody but yourself.

MRS. SNIP: Where is he, Abram, 'tis all over Daughter; We are made forever:—I'll go to him.

[*Exit* MRS. SNIP *P. S.*]

ABRAM: Miss Dolly,—Miss Dolly—shall we fetch a Walk together this fine Evening.

DOLLY: Fetch a Walk, no, I won't fetch a Walk; I beg Abraham, that you'll keep to your Shop; and not talk so familiarly to Me.—Fetch a Walk—I don't think ever to walk again.

ABRAM: Heigh to Pass, Whats the matter now, Miss Dolly: You ben't false hearted like the great Ladies be ye.

DOLLY: But I be though; don't talk to me—Go and mind Your Business.

ABRAM: Heres for you indeed, You told me another Story Last Saturday night, when I was kissing & Toying with you in my Masters Hall above Stairs. But those happy Hours are past, they are gone to be sure. And so if you are chang'd, why I am chang'd.—Your Servant—Your Servant—Your Servant, Miss Dolly.— [*Exit P. S.*]
[*ACT.*]

DOLLY: I have begun pretty well with him. I'll quite turn him off the next time. Not but I'll do him some kindness. Perhaps I may make him one of my Footmen. He's genteel, and, I shall like to have him about me—O Law, if I should be Lady Doll Snip, the first thing I do, I'll be half Lame, & Half Blind like Lady Totteridge, and I'll have a long train Draggling after me, which when I want to be Smart I shall tuck under my Arm thus, and Jig it away, my Teeth shall be white as Ivory, & my Cheeks as Red as a Cherry. I'm not an Ugly Girl. I know that—I won't be stuff'd up twice or thrice a year at Holiday Time at the Top of the Playhouse, among Folks that laugh and cry, just as they feel. Then I'll carry my Head as high, and have as High a Head as the best of 'em, and it shall be all set out with Curls—It shall be too high to go in at any Door, without Stooping, and so broad that I must always go in Sideways; Then I shall Keep a Chair with a Cupola o' top to hold my Feather Head in, and I shall be carried in it by Day, and by Night, Dingle, Dangle, Bobbing and Nodding, all the way I go. Then I shall sit in the side Boxes, among by equals, Laugh, talk loud—mind nothing —Stare at the low People in the Galleries, without ever looking at them—Thus.—Then they'll hate me as much as I shall my old Acquaintance—What a Life shall I lead, when I'm a fine Lady, I'll be as fine as any of 'em, and will be turn'd quite topsy turvey as well as the best of 'em.

Act Ends.   [*Exit.*]

Drop.   ABRAM *Dresses*

Act 3ᵈ Scene continues.

Enter Dolly Snip OP

Was there ever any thing so unlucky. I was this
Morning out of my Senses, and thought my Father
a great Man, and myself a fine Lady — and now
my Dreams out — My Father has lost his Head,
My Mother is breaking her Heart, and what is
worse than all, I must work for my Living — it is
a sad Thing, a terrible thing to be oblig'd to work
when one has set ones mind upon lying a Bed
and thinking of nothing, then there's Abram too,
I wish I had not turn'd him of — I must not let
him go, I know he can't help loving me — and he
knows his Interest — So I will e'en marry him; —
Make my Mother give up the Shop to him —
Allow her a trifle to maintain her, and take
the Business into my own Hands — I can't
think of any thing better at present.   *Abram* (3)

Enter Sukey Chitterlin. PS

Sukey
Cousin Dolly! Cousin Dolly — Cousin Dolly.

Dolly
Lord what a noise you make; always Roaring
and Romping.

Sukey.

Garrick's *Harlequin's Invasion*, III, i. From the MS. in the Barton-
Ticknor Collection of the Boston Public Library.

ACT III
Drop Chab^r
Enter DOLLY SNIP *OP*

Was there ever anything so unlucky. I was this Morning
out of my Senses, and thought my Father a great Man, and
myself a fine Lady—and now my Dreams out—My Father
has lost his Head; my Mother is breaking her Heart, and
what is worse than all, I must work for my Living—it is a
sad Thing, a terrible thing to be oblig'd to work when one
has set ones mind upon lying a Bed and thinking of nothing, then there's Abram too. I wish I had not turn'd him
of — I must not let him go, I know he can't help loving
me—and he knows his Interest—So I will e'en marry him;
—Make my Mother give up the Shop to him—Allow her
a trifle to maintain her, and take the Business into my own
Hands—I can't think of any thing better at present.

[(3) ABRAM]

[*Enter* SUKEY CHITTERLIN. *P. S.*]

SUKEY: Cousin Dolly!—Cousin Dolly—Cousin Dolly.

DOLLY: Lord what a Noise you make; always Roaring
and Romping.

SUKEY: Why would not you have me merry & in Spirits.

DOLLY: I wou'd not have you so boisterous, Ma'am.

SUKEY: I am sorry to see you so frumpish, Miss Dolly. I
came for a little advice; Your Abram, since you turn'd him
off, has made proposals to me—Now as we have always
open'd our Hearts to each other Cousin, and you are my
most intimate Friend—I want to know if you think it a
good Match for me, He's a handsome Man to be sure tho'

he's a little of the Rakish Cast—I don't like him the worse for it—I have a Turn for high Fun myself—Eh, Cousin.

DOL: Then you'll be both ruin'd—You are too Young a little, waiting will do you no harm.

SUKEY: Egad I don't know that Cousin—I'm sure it will do me no good—If He don't think me too Young I'm sure I won't, I may wait longer, and fare worse, mayn't I Cousin.

DOLLY: But such Things should not be done in a hurry Cousin.

SUKEY: One may do worse things in a hurry Cousin, and so if you have no better Advice to give, I'll e'en follow my own.

DOLLY: You are grown very glib of your Tongue Miss.

SUKEY: You left it off Miss, and I took it up—I make a shift with your leavings—Abram, among the rest I'm not proud and fantastical Miss.

DOLLY: You are very impertinent Miss, and deserve to have your Ears box'd.

SUKEY: The sooner the better, for my fingers hate to be idle

DOLLY: Get out of the Room, you saucy flirt you.

SUKEY: You fancy yourself a Lady in good earnest. But pride will have a fall. I know you hate me. And I know the Reason of it, I happen to be handsomer than Somebody, and have as much money as Somebody, and I was Toasted last Friday Night at the Spouting Club, before Somebody—and all this gives pain to Somebody, who from thinking herself a Lady forsooth—is become No-body, and so my Lady Doll, Somebody—No-body—Your humble

Servant—but here comes your Abram. My Abram, I mean —Lord, he's a fine Man, and looks so Rakish, and so amorous—Oh 'tis a Charming bewitching Fellow.

[Enter ABRAM. *Dress'd. PS]*

ABRAM: Come, Miss Sukey, will you fetch a Walk with Me. I did not know your Ladyship was here; or I shou'd not have Intruded—Come Miss Sukey.   *[going]*

SUKEY: There's Wit, and a fleer for you—Oh! he's a charming Fellow, and a perfect Satyr.

DOLLY: Mr. Abram, May I have the favour of speaking a word to you.

ABRAM: With *Me,* my Lady,—no my Lady—I know my Distance, which you have taught me my Lady—Keep to your Shop Abraham & don't talk so familiarly to me— Fetch a Walk! I don't think ever to Walk again—I'll keep my distance my Lady. Come Miss Chitterlin—I know my distance my Lady.

[(4) BOUNCE, GASCONADE *in Chains*]

SUKEY: What a Satyr he is; I'm glad I've got Him.

DOLLY: Pray let me speak with you Cousin.

SUKEY: Oh not for the World my Lady.

[(5) GOALER, *bunch of Keys*]

BOTH: Ha! ha! ha!

DOLLY: Why then I must tell you Sukey Chitterlin, that you are a treacherous, base Girl, to take my Sweetheart from me.

ABRAM: That's Me.—I knew she'd repent it.   *[Struts]*

SUKEY: And I must tell you, Miss Madam, My Lady

Dol. Snip, that you falsify yourself to say so—You bid me take him so you did, and I have taken him. And I'll keep him too—Shan't I Abram.

[(6) HARLEQUIN, *wine etc Ready*]

ABRAM: That you shall, Body, and Soul of me, Miss Sukey, and no bad bargain neither.

DOLLY: Go, you poor, pitiful, low-minded——

ABRAM [*x to Centre & back*]: As good a Man as your Father, Miss, aye and better too; for I've got my Head upon my Shoulders. [*Struts*]

DOLLY: Yes, yes, you have a Head, and it will be finely furnished shortly.

SUKEY: And so it shall, Madam,—He shall want for nothing that I can help him to.

ABRAM: I shall want nothing that she can help me to. [*Struts*]. Come Wife, that is to be; don't let us lose time with a Mad Lady, Your Servant my Lady Doll, ha! ha! ha!

SUKEY: Your Ladyships most obedient.

BOTH: Ha! ha! ha!

ABRAM: I knew she'd repent at last.

[*Struts out with Sukey. PS*]

DOLLY: I am mad indeed, I cou'd tear both their Eyes out. A low bred foolish Girl in my Situation wou'd run distracted—But I don't mind it no more than a pins point not I. I despise and laugh at it, he, he, he. I can't bear it neither—I must go and cry a little to Recover myself.

[*Exit OP.*]

[40]

B. B. W. SCENE *a Prison. Table to Change & Sink.*
BOUNCE & GASCONADE *Discover'd.*

BOUNCE: Is not this a most lamentable Situation for a Man of my Soul and Ambition, I who have thinn'd Nations,—Mow'd down Armies, to be hang'd at last for killing a Taylor; It is not Death, 'tis the disgrace, the dishonour is all my concern.

GASCONADE: En Verite inteed that no concerns me at all. If they will give me my Life, I will put my disgrace in my Pocket.

BOUNCE: Is there no way to get out of this damn'd hole. I had always a good Hand at getting into Prisons, I wish I knew as well how to get out of One—Egad I have it. My dear Friend, You shall help me up to that Window there, and then I can easily make my Escape over the Top of the next House. [(7) MRS. SNIP]

GASCON: Eh Bien, my dear Friend, and vat must I do den, Eh!

BOUNCE: Faith thats true, why you shall stay here, and let 'em know that I am gone; but that I will certainly come again when they want me. [8. Mr. SNIP, TURNKEY]

GASCON: I very much tank you for dat, Monsr. Bounce, Non, non, If I must be hang'd, mon amie; I love that my dear friend shou'd keep a me Compagnie.

[*Enter* JAILOR *P. S.* (*Bunch of Keys*)]

Well, Gentlemen, I bring you Good News, Good news.

BOUNCE: What a Reprieve.

GASCON: Vat a Reprieve.

[41]

JAILOR: A Reprieve, no, no, You'll certainly be hang'd and to-morrow too, but the good News I have brought you is, that your friends have got Permission for a Fryar to attend you, and here behold your Father & Comforter.

[*P S Enter* HARLEQN (*like a Fryar*)]

HARLEQ: Peace be with the Afflicted. Jailor a chair. & a Bottle of Sack. The Body requires Rest & Refreshment. [*Ext Jailor P. S.*] As you are under Misfortunes, what I am going to say shall be utter'd with the utmost gentleness & Humanity. You are without doubt Gentlen I speak it from my Soul, a couple of horrid Rascals.

GASCON: Dat is very gentile indeed.

BOUNCE: And very true [*aside.*]

[*Enter* JAILOR *with Wine P. S.*]

HARLEQ: Gentlemen to your Speedy Execution.

GASCON: Je vous remercie, He's very complaisant indeed!

HARLEQ: Another to your Repentence, and then to Business.

GASCON: Begar you vas sent here to give us Consolation, and you take all de Consolation yourself.

HARLEQ: Son I shall give you spiritual Consolation, but in the first Place, I must Examine the Sullen Sinner, Of what Religion are you?

BOUNCE: None.

HARLEQ: Of what Religion are you.

GASCON: Whatever you please.

HARLEQ: 'Tis really a pity you shou'd Suffer, for you have

[42]

been both exceedingly well Educated—will you confess anything?

BOUNCE: No.

HARLEQ: Will you confess, Sir?

GASCO: I do confess, and profess, too Sir: that I have no great desire to be hang'd.

[Enter MRS. SNIP *P. S. D.]*

MRS. SNIP: Let me come! Let me come; and let me indulge myself with the Sight of poor Joes Murderers—Oh! you base, base Villains to deprive so civil and peaceable a Woman as I am, of as good a Husband and as good a Workman—I can't bear the thoughts of it—Let me come at 'em—Let me come at 'em. If I were in a passion now, I cou'd tear their Execratious Eyes out—Well, poor Joe, thou wert a little too Domineering and Robustious sometimes, But my quiet Temper soon appeas'd thee; Thy Passion was soon over—I shall never get such another for my purpose. *[Enter* SNIP *PS]* A Ghost! a Ghost—I shall die —I shall die.—

BOUNCE: No Ghost! no Ghost!—I shall live! I shall live! 'Tis He himself.

GASCON: Ah! Je vive aussi. I am alive too.

BOUNCE: Off with my Chains—I'll swear to his Face.

GASCON: Ouy, I'll Swear to his Face, for I did Cut off his Head.

JAILOR: Where have you been Joe?

SNIP: I have been murder'd Neighbour Padlock.

[43]

Mrs. Snip: And are you really Flesh and Blood. Let me feel You—Come nearer—Don't touch me, if you are not a Man—He's warm—Kiss me,—Kiss me again. Tis my Joe, I know 'tis he.—I am glad to see you again; but I am sorry you came back so soon too. had you but stay'd a day longer, these two would have been hang'd for Murdering of you.

Jailor: But since things have happen'd otherwise, I'll e'en release my Prisoners.

[*takes off their Chains and throws 'em off PS.*]

Gascon: De tout Mon Coeur.

Bounce: Huzza!

Turnkey [*within (Prompter)*]: Lock up all the Doors, —Bar up all the Windows—Keep a good look out the back way.

Jailor: Whats the matter Turnkey?

Turnkey [*Prompter*]: Look about ye, Harlequins in the Prison.

Jailor: The Devil he is, that would be a prize indeed.

Bounce: Now Monsieur! Now's our Time.

Gascon: Pardonnez Moi,—I vil burn my Finger no more.

Harl: Give me some Sack Oh I shall faint—I shall faint. Harlequins in the Prison.

Mrs. Snip: Poor Soul! Poor Soul!

Snip: May I never handle Needle again, if this is not the Blackamoor Gentleman, that sow'd my Head on.

All: 'Tis Harlequin! 'Tis Harlequin himself.

Jailor: Now for it Boys, the Prize is our own.

[They advance to seize him]

Tr. Bell to change Table—To the Devil.
Trap Bell to Sink Table.

GASCON: Vat is all dis, I am fright out of my Wits!

MRS. SNIP: Mercy on us, they are raising the Devil here!

BOUNCE: Oh! Oh! Oh!   *[Music in the Orchestra]*

Trap Bell—Border Bell—Wing Bell.
Prison Returns. 1st Transparency

SNIP: We are all bewitch'd! I shall certainly lose my Head again!

JAILOR: Why I am in my own Jail again.

BOUNCE: And I'll get out of it as fast as I can.

TURNKEY *[without]*: Bring him along. Bring him along.

BOUNCE: What have we got here? My Father and Confessor.   *[Harlequin brought on by MERCURY Pd.]*

GASCON: Eh! Monsieur Consolation, are you caught, with all your Tricks, you dam black Dog.

MERCURY: Come, come, strip Hypocrisy lin'd with Folly. *[Draws off the Fryars Gown—HARLEQ: tries to Escape.]* Not so fast Monsieur Harlequin, I have Heels shall Match Yours.—Run—fly—Swim—Leap—I am after you and if you are for fighting, I have a Weapon here. Ecce Signum. *[Shewing his Caduceus].*

GASCON: There is Consolation for You—Mon bon Pere.

MERCURY: In a true Glass I'll set to View
          Your Fate and that of all your Crew.

[45]

Hence you prophane without delay.
This Scene is not for You—Away.

Exeunt SNIP, MRS. SNIP—GASCONADE, BOUNCE &
JAILOR *OP*

MERCURY *waves his Caduceus (Music in Orchestra)*

Tr. Bell   Border Bell   Wing Bell.
Prison Sinks.

The Second Transparency appear Representing the Powers
of Pantimime going to Attack Mount Parnassus. A
Storm comes on destroys the Fleet. (When the Ship
Splits—*Whistle*) *Rock Flat. Shuts up Transparency.*

MERCURY:
Hear Earthly Proteus, hear great Jove's decree
His Thunder Sleeps, and thus he speaks by me
Descend to Earth be Sportive as before
Wait on the Muses Train, like Fools of Yore
Beware encroachment and invade no more.

HARL: *Stands on Front Trap OP*

MERCURY *waves his Caduceus.*
Tr. Bell   Wing Bell   Border Bell.
Temple of the Gods.

MERCURY: Now let immortal Shakespear rise
Ye Sons of Taste Adore him
As from the Sun each Vapour flies
Let Folly sink before him.

[*Wave Caduceus*]

Trap Bell
Shakespear Rises: Harlequin Sinks

[46]

SONG

Thrice happy th' Nation that Shakespear has charm'd
More happy the Bosom his Genius has warm'd
Ye Children of Nature, of Fashion, and Whim
He painted you all, all join to praise him
    Come away, come away, come away.
    His Genius calls and you must obey.

At the Chorus many of Shakespears Characters Enter. P. S.
&OP Also the three Graces who Dance to the Repeat.

(2d)

To praise him ye Fairies and Genii Repair
He knew where you haunted in Earth, or in Air
No Phantom so subtle could glide from his View
The Wings of his Fancy were swifter than You.
    Come away, Come away.
    His Genius Calls and you must obey.

At the Chorus several Fairies & Genii Enter.
The Fairies Dance to the Repeat.

3d.

Ye Britons may Fancy ne'er lead you astray
Nor e'er through your Senses your Reason betray
By your Love to the Bard may your wisdom be known
Nor injure his Fame to the loss of your own.
    Come away, Come away.
    His Genius calls and we must away.

During the 3d. *Verse the Figure Dancers Enter. When*
over, the Grand Dance is Executed while the Chorus
is Sung & Repeated.

            Ring   Curtain
                Finis

NOTES

HARLEQUIN'S INVASION

PAGE 11. 2d *Grove*. This indicates the groove in which the flats were run. They used to come together in the centre, and the wings were pushed on at the sides to match them. The distance between the grooves facing the various entrances was usually six feet, the first entrance from the Proscenium wing to the curtain line being narrower—about four feet.

PAGE 11. 2. BOUNCE *a Stick*. Garrick, throughout this MS., indicated the appearance of characters and change of scene somewhat before these were due. This was done probably to give the actors time to prepare for their appearance on the stage and the stage-hands time to make the necessary arrangements for the next change of scene. In the MS., these preliminary warnings appear as side notes in the margin (See facsimile pages). In the present edition, however, they have been placed, for typographical reasons, within the limits of the type page.

PAGE 11. *Enter* BOUNCE *Pd*. Pd. means prompt door. There was always a door in the prompt.

PAGE 12. *O. P.* means opposite prompt entrances.

PAGE 12. *P. S.* means prompt side, whatever side the prompter was on, irrespective of right or left.

PAGE 13. *French Trick*. This might have reference to the war then raging between England and France for supremacy in America and India. The year 1759 (the year that saw the production of Garrick's *Harlequin's Invasion*) was signalized by the great number of British victories over the French, the most important of which was the defeat of the French army at Quebec. This might also refer to Harlequin's tricks. Harlequin is here regarded as a Frenchman.

[51]

PAGE 13. *Bor. Bell* and *Ws Bell*. In the early days of
the theatre, no ceilings were used, but borders were hung
in front of the grooves in each entrance: sky, foliage, or
drapery, to meet the subject of each scene. With the change
of each scene, the border bell was sounded to indicate that
the borders were to be changed from exteriors to interiors
or vice versa as is the case with this present scene (from
Charing Cross to a Chamber). The same applies to the
wings as to the borders.

PAGE 15. [*x to P. S.*] means crosses to prompt side.

PAGE 16. 2. *En O. P.* signifies the second entrance opposite prompt. There were about six or seven entrances on
either side of the stage.

PAGE 16. *O. P.* 1st *Ent*—Opposite prompt first entrance.

PAGE 18. 4 *G.* Fourth Groove. See note for 2d Grove,
page 11.

PAGE 23. (*x to O. P.*), crosses to opposite prompt.

PAGE 24. *Bar Bell*. Mr. Seymour's explanation of this
stage direction is as follows: "In the early theatres—England and this country—each theatre had a *bar* or *refreshment* room on each floor—the price of drinks conforming
to the price of seats paid on said floors. We had these *bars*
in the theatres within my remembrance—and they were in
full blast in London when I was last there—twelve years
ago. The prompter used to ring the bell a few minutes before the rising of the curtain to bring the people back to
their seats. The same holds to-day—they are rung in from
the smoking rooms."

PAGE 27. *Curtain Bell*. Bell to lower the curtain, marking the end of the act.

PAGE 28. *deep*. The MS. at this point reads:

And tho' shallow yet seem to be dark

but *dark* gives neither rhyme nor reason. Reason demands a word antithetical to *shallow*; rhyme demands a word consonant with *sleep*. The combined requirements seem to be best met by the word here substituted—*deep*. Presumably, *dark* in the MS. is a clerical error of Garrick or his copyist, an error easily made in transcription if, in the copying of line 3, the eye chanced first to light on the last word of line 5.

PAGE 31. (*x to P. S.*). Crosses to prompt side.

PAGE 31. *P. D.* See page 11.

PAGE 32. *"Ill carry my Head as high etc."* This refers to the extraordinarily high coiffures of the fashionable ladies of the day. To secure comfort while traveling in their sedan chairs, the ladies were obliged to have cupolas built on top of these chairs to hold their high head-dresses.

PAGE 33. *"Then I shall sit etc."* This is Garrick's hit at the behavior of the ladies of the *beau monde* at the theatre.

PAGE 37. *Drop Chabr.* This stage direction probably means drop curtain representing a chamber.

PAGE 38. *Spouting Club*. Declaiming Club.

PAGE 41. *B. B. W.* Border Bell and Wings Bell.

PAGE 43. *P. S. D.* Prompt side down.

THE JUBILEE

Mr Garrick reciting the Ode; in honour of Shakespear, at the Jubilee at Stratford: with the Musical Accompaniments &c.

From the print in the Theatre Collection of the Harvard University Library. This print appeared in the *Town and Country Magazine*, London, September, 1769.

INTRODUCTION

T HE year 1769 was made memorable in the history of the English drama by the famous Stratford Jubilee, which Garrick arranged and conducted at Stratford-upon-Avon in honor of his darling Shakespeare. This celebration lasted three days. The circumstances leading to the Jubilee and the events themselves are so familiar that a detailed account of these is here unnecessary: but a brief outline of what took place prior to and during the Stratford festivities may prove acceptable.

The entire Jubilee celebration centers around the famous mulberry-tree, which was said to have been planted by the poet's own hand in the garden of New Place, his home in Stratford-upon-Avon. In 1753, New Place came into the possession of the Reverend Francis Gastrell, Vicar of Frodsham in Cheshire, and three years later, this clergyman ordered the venerable mulberry-tree to be cut down because it overshadowed the house and rendered it damp and uninhabitable. This action on the part of the Reverend Mr. Gastrell roused the anger of the Stratfordians (to whom everything connected with their own Shakespeare was sacred) to such a pitch that they drove him out of the town and solemnly swore never to endure another Gastrell in their midst.

The remains of what was once the favorite tree of the

immortal Shakespeare were now bought by a carpenter, who cut and moulded the wood into various objects. That part of the mulberry-tree which was procured by the Corporation of Stratford, was turned into an elaborately carved box in which the officials placed the freedom of their town and presented it to Garrick with a request that he send them a "bust, statue, or picture of Shakespeare" and a picture of himself to place in their new Town Hall so that the "memory of both may be perpetuated together."[1]

Highly flattered by this compliment, Garrick lost no time in sending to the Corporation not only a portrait of Shakespeare, painted by Benjamin Wilson, but also a statue of the poet by Roubiliac, together with a full-length portrait of himself by Gainsborough. It was this interchange of compliments on the part of the Corporation of the town of Shakespeare's birth and the great interpreter of some of Shakespeare's most important characters, that led to the organization of the Stratford Jubilee, which began with great éclat at day-break of Wednesday, September sixth, and ended in a somewhat dampened atmosphere long after midnight of September the eighth.

Elaborate preparations, such as the building of a large amphitheatre in imitation of the Rotunda of the Ranelagh Gardens, and the enveloping of Shakespeare's birthplace and also the Town Hall in emblematic transparencies, were made; but nothing was done in the way of preparing proper accommodations for the large number of visitors who were to pour into Stratford from all directions. Hence, the great influx of guests found Stratford wholly unprepared to minister to their convenience. This situation is excel-

---

[1] Boaden, *Garrick Correspondence*, 1831, I, 322.

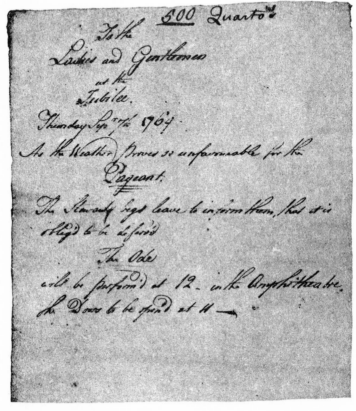

Garrick's order to his printer for 500 copies of a hand-bill announcing the postponement of the pageant of Shakespearean characters. From the MS. in the Theatre Collection of the Harvard University Library.

lently pictured in the post-chaise and the inn scenes of Garrick's dramatic entertainment *The Jubilee*.

Serenades, public breakfasts, ordinaries, concerts, the performance of Dr. Arne's Oratorio *Judith*, Garrick's recitation of his own Ode on the dedication of the new Town Hall and the erection of a statue of Shakespeare, the musical parts of which were composed and conducted by Dr. Arne, balls, and masquerades, such was the round of entertainments enjoyed by the visitors to the Stratford Jubilee. The pageant of Shakespearean characters through the streets of Stratford, one of the principal events of the celebration, was abandoned on account of the violent downpour, which began on the second day and continued through the third. The rain also spoiled the grand display of fireworks which Garrick's friend Angelo had so carefully prepared. To make matters worse, the Avon overflowed its banks and flooded all the approaches to the amphitheatre. Planks had to be laid to enable the guests arriving for the masquerade to alight from their carriages.

Through all these festivities strutted Garrick, the Steward of the Jubilee, with his mulberry wand and gold-framed mulberry medallion, which had been presented to him by the officials of the town, and which he wore throughout the celebration on a ribbon about his neck.

Garrick's dramatic trifle, *The Jubilee*, was designed as a vehicle for the representation of the pageant of Shakespearean characters, which had been intended for the Stratford festival, but which, on account of the heavy rainfall, had been dispensed with. In this piece, Garrick ridicules the whole Jubilee affair. Although the Corporation of Stratford sanctioned the festivities which Garrick con-

[63]

ducted in their little town, the Stratfordians themselves were hostile to the impious invaders of their sacred realm. This hostility of the townspeople to these pilgrims at Shakespeare's shrine; the imposition practiced by the Stratfordians on their guests; their outrageous extortions; the crowded conditions at the inn; the pageant and the rain: all these incidents, embellished with a goodly portion of mulberry wood, go to make up Garrick's rather enjoyable little piece *The Jubilee*. It was produced at the Drury Lane Theatre on the 14th of October, 1769,[2] and played to crowded houses for ninety-two consecutive nights.

The players who took part in this after-piece were King, who played Ralph; Moody, the Irishman; Vernon, a ballad-singer; Parsons, the Ostler; Mrs. Baddeley and Miss Radley, country-girls; Mrs. Love, Margery Jarvis; and Mrs. Bradshaw, Goody Benson. Garrick walked in the pageant as Benedick in *Much Ado About Nothing* to Miss Pope's Beatrice. Mrs. Barry was the Tragic Muse, and Mrs. Abington represented her more joyous sister, Thalia.

Genest says that the Drury Lane manuscript of Garrick's *The Jubilee* was "burnt with the theatre in 1809."[3] The text which follows these introductory remarks, however, proves Genest's statement to be false. This manuscript was in the possession of John Philip Kemble and later formed part of the Duke of Devonshire's Collection. As has already been stated in the Preface to this volume, this Kemble-Devonshire Collection passed, in 1914, into the hands of its present owner, Mr. Henry Edwards Huntington.

[2] Genest, V, 256.
[3] *Ibid.*

THE JUBILEE

The Jubilee

Scene 1. an Old Womans House

An old Woman asleep in a Wicker Chair
a Bottle by her.

2 Old Woman (without)

Goody. Benson! Goody Benson! what an't you
up Woman? tis near five o'clock!

1. Old Wom: (waking)

Bless me! who's there? ... I'm frighted out of my
wits — who calls?

2 O. Wom

Tis I, 'tis I neighbour — Margery Jarvis — let me
speak with you.

1. O. Wom

ay, ay, & thank you too Margery.
(puts the bottle under the chair
& goes to the door)

2 O. Wom

What are you up Dame?

1. O. Wom

Up Woman; why I hanno' been a bed not I — nor

SCENE I. *an Old Womans House.*

An old Woman asleep in a Wicker Chair a Bottle by her.

2D OLD WOMAN [*without*]: Goody Benson! Goody Benson! what an't you up woman? tis near five o'clock!

1ST OLD WOM. [*waking*]: Bless me! who's there? I'm frighted out of my wits—who calls?

2D O. WOM.: 'Tis I, 'tis I neighbour—Margery Jarvis— let me speak with you.

1ST O. WOM.: Ay, ay, & thank you too Margery.
        [*puts the bottle under the Chair & goes to the door.*]

2D O. WOM.: What are you up Dame?

1ST O. WOM.: Up Woman, why I hanno' been a bed not I —nor canno' rest since this racket begun—I durst not lay me down, but was taking a little nap in my chair, when you knock'd at the door—I verily think Neighbour, this Jubillo, will be death o' me.

2D O. WOM.: I canno' rest neither, not I—I wish twas all over, and these Londoners were well out of Town, one is not safe in ones bed,—I canno' guess what they'd be at.—

1ST O. WOM.: I darn't trust 'em neither. — I have not pull'd off my Cloaths this week—but doze, doze in my Chair.—I wish they have not more in their Yeads, than we are aware of.——

2D O. WOM.: Our Ralph swears theres mischief in hond —and the poor soul has ne'er been his own Mon,—since the Jubillo was talk'd of—he verily believes—that the Pope is at bottom on't all.

[69]

RALPH [*peeps in*]: Introth, and so I do Neighbour.

BOTH O. WOM.: Mercy on us! who's there?——

2D O. WOM.: Why would you startle us so Ralph, in these frightful times——I'm glad you are come tho'—you are up I see, as well as us.

RALPH: Is this a time to lye a bed, when the Town may be flown away with, for ought we know?—I should not like to wake, and find my self a hundred Miles off—and so I don't sleep at all, nor will I, till the Devil has done his worst.——

1ST O. WOM.: Prithee don't talk so Ralph—you set my back a aching, and I tremble every Joint of me.

RALPH: And not without Reason Neighbour.—I'll be hang'd up alive (and may be for ought I know) but there is some plot a foot with this Jubillo.

BOTH O. WOM.: Bless us!

RALPH: Why there are a hundred Taylors in Town—! and all from London—'tis certainly a Plot of the Jews and Papishes.——

1ST O. WOM.: Terrible indeed!——

RALPH: Why Dame, the Taylors, and Barbers alone wou'd breed a famine—then they have brought Cannon Guns down with them, and a mortal deal of Gunpowder; what's Gunpowder for?—to blow us all up in a fillip!—another powder plot, Heav'n preserve us!—little Dolly Dobson will take her bible Oath, that She saw fifty Devils at work in Farmer Thornton's Barn, & Cow-house!—she has been partly out of her mind ever since.——

2D O. WOM.: They are at the same work in the Colledge here,—such a Cargo of all sorts of Conjuration!——

RALPH: O yes, they keep all their Hobgoblins there—and if they're let loose about the Town, not all our Parsons preaching, will drive them out again.

1ST O. WOM.: P'rithee Ralph, does know why they build such a large great *round house* in the Meadow for?——

RALPH: Why to drive all us poor Folks in, to be sure,— like Cattle into a Pound—then lock us in, while they may be firing the Town, and running away with & ravish, ay that's what they will—Ravish Man, Woman & Child— how can one sleep, with such thoughts in ones head!

2D O. WOM.: Ravishing O Law!—and yet were there no Mischief afoot—there's a power of Money to be got,—I might have let my little room for a good sum an' I would —but auld you said I, Gold may be bought too dear—and yet I'de have ventur'd for t' other Guinea.

RALPH: More shame for you!—do you think they would make such a rout, about our Shakespur the Poet, if they had not other things in their pates?—I knew something was abrewing, when they wou'd not let his Image alone in the Church, but had the Shew People to paint it in such fine Colours, to look like a Popish Saint—ay, ay!—that was the beginning of it all.

1ST O. WOM.: Have you seen Ralph, the Mon, that is the ring leader of the Jubillo?—who is to fly about the Town by Conjuration?——

2D O. WOM.: Ay, the Mon that came from London—The Steward as they call 'en—have you seen he Ralph?

[71]

RALPH: Yes, I ha' seen him—not much to be seen tho'—
I did not care to come too near him—he's not so big as I,
but a great deal plumper,—he's auld enough to be wiser
too,—but he knows what he's about, I warrant 'en—he has
brought the Pipers and 'Ecod, he'll make us pay for 'em—
let him alone for that—he's a long Yead of his own.——
[*Cannon fires without*]

ALL: [*starting & trembling*] Lud have mercy upon us!
[*Cannon fires again*]

RALPH: Now they are at it—[*Cannon fires again*] We
shall all be blown up! Lud have mercy upon us! [*Cannon
fires again*] I'll go & take a peep at a distance & bring you
word if I see any Mischief. [*Cannon fires again*]

1. O. W.: Ralph! don't leave us alone. We'll take a Peep
too——

2D O. W.: Have they begun ravishing, Ralph?

RALPH: O Lud have mercy upon us! Nay, nay, don't you
be frighten'd—what the Devil shou'd you be frighten'd
for? [*Cannon fires again*] O Lud! of Mercy upon us!
[*Ex. trembling & much frighten'd.*]

SCENE II. *The Street, with a Post chaise on one side.*
Enter Musicians wth Singers in Dominos, to give a
Serenade—Ladies looks out at a window.

AIR

Let Beauty with the Sun arise,
    To Shakespeare tribute pay,
With heavenly smiles, and Sparkling Eyes,
    Give Grace and Lustre to the day.

[72]

2.

Each smile she gives protects his name:
  What face shall dare to frown?
Not Envy's self can blast the fame,
  Which Beauty deigns to crown.

IRISHMAN [*peeping out of the chaise window*]: What a plague do you mean there below, with your noise, and your Music, and your colour'd Surplusses,—disturbing Gentlemen in their beds before they are got to Sleep?

MUSICIAN: Oh Sir, this is part of the Jubilee, Sir.

I. MAN: Yes, and I dare say you think it very Entertaining—I could not get to the Jubilee 'till twelve O'Clock last Night, and I walk'd about the Streets for two hours to get a bed, and a bit of Supper, but the Devil a toothful of neither one nor t'other could I get—and so I was forc'd to take lodgings in the first floor of this Postchaise, at a half Crown a head, and here they have cramm'd a bedfellow with me, into the bargain—not being able to lye down upright in my bed; I could not get a wink of Sleep 'till you were pleas'd to wake me with your damn'd Scraping and Caterwauling; I never had such a Night in all my days; and is this what you call a Jubilee?—It's truly worth while to travel from Dublin to be sure of such a recreation. But what is your Jubilee Honey? 'tis full time to know.

MUSICIAN: If your honour pleases to come out, I'll sing you a Song about the Jubilee.

I. MAN: With all my heart fait, for I am ready drest, tho' I'm in bed you see—and if you'll do me the honour to open my chamber door, you'll greatly oblige me?

[73]

[*Musician opens the door & he comes out.*] Mr. Musicioner, I'm your humble Servant—but stay let me shut the chamber door upon my bedfellow that he may not catch cold;—Upon my conscience I was forc'd to make a Night Cap of my wig, that the hair may keep me warm—and now pray inform me, what is this same Jubilee, that I am come so far to see, and know nothing of the matter.

MUSICIAN:

> This is Sir a Jubilee
> Crowded without Company
> Riot without Jollity
> That's a Jubilee
> > Thus 'tis night & day Sir
> > I hope that you will stay Sir
> > > To see our Jubilee.

2.

> On the road Such Crosses Sir
> Cursing Jolts & tossing Sir
> Posting without Horses Sir
> > Thus 'tis etc.

3.

> Odes Sir without Poetry
> Music without Melody
> Singing without Harmony.
> > Thus 'tis etc.

4.

> Holes to thrust your head in Sir
> Lodgings without Bedding Sir
> Beds as if They'd Lead in Sir
> > Thus 'tis etc.

5.

Blankets without Sheeting Sir
Dinners without Eating Sir
Not without much cheating Sir
    Thus 'tis etc.

I. MAN: 'Tis a comical kind of a Song to be sure & you did not stale it from what they say of little Kilkenny—there we have—

    Fire without Smoak
    Wit without Joke
    Air without fog
    Land without bog
    Men without heads
    Lodging without beds.

O No! that's your Jubilee Rig, Ecce Signum [*pointing to the Postchaise*] We have——

    Water without Mud,
    Beds without bug,
    Pudding without Eggs
    Rabbets without legs.

MUSICIAN: Rabbets without legs?

I. MAN: Yes, Rabbets without legs—welsh ones—Besides, Rabbets fore Legs are two of 'em Wings Honey—Then I was upon you now. But what are we to have next? for I went to the great big Inn, where all the plays are writ upon the doors, and so I thought to see a play, and pop'd my head into *Much Ado about Nothing* and there was nothing at all but the Steward with his Mulberry box upon his breast, speaking his fine Ode to music.

[75]

2 BALLAD SINGERS [*behind*]: This is entitled and call'd—
O Rare Warwickshire!

MUSICIAN: O Sir, here's something will rouse you if you
are not awake—here they come!——

Enter BALLAD SINGERS, *etc.*

MAN-BALLAD SINGER (*Vernon*):

     Ye Warwickshire lads, and ye lasses,
     See what at our Jubilee passes,
     Come revel away, rejoice and be Glad,
     For the lad of all lads was a Warwickshire lad,
        Warwickshire lad,
        All be Glad!
     For the Lad of all lads was a Warwickshire lad.

WOMAN (*Dibdin*):

     Be proud of the Charms of your Country,
     Where Nature has lavish'd her bounty,
     Where much she has giv'n, and some to be spar'd,
     For the Bard of all bards, was a Warwickshire bard,
        Warwickshire bard,
        Never pair'd
     For the Bard of all Bards was a Warwickshire bard.

MAN:

     Old Ben, Thomas Otway, John Dryden,
     And half a Score more, we take pride in,
     Of Famous Will Congreve, we boast too the Skill,
     But the Will of all Wills was a Warwickshire Will;
        Warwickshire Will,
        Matchless still!
     For the Will of all Wills was a Warwickshire Will.

WOMAN:

> As Ven'son is very Inviting,
> To steal it our bard took delight in,
> To Make his friends Merry he never was lag,
> And the Wag of all Wags was a Warwickshire Wag,
>> Warwickshire Wag,
>> Ever brag,
> For the Wag of all Wags was a Warwickshire Wag.

MAN:

> There never was seen such a creature,
> Of all she was worth he robb'd nature;
> He took all her Smiles, and he took all her Grief,
> And the thief of all thieves, was a Warwickshire
>> thief,
>>> Warwickshire thief
>>> He's the Chief,
> For the thief of all thieves was a Warwickshire
>> thief.
> He took etc. [*Ex. Singing.*]

I. MAN: The devil burn me—but I believe you are *all*
Tieves.

>> Jubilee thief,
>> 'Tis my belief,
> The thief of all thieves is a Jubilee thief.
>>>> [*Ex. Singing.*]

SCENE III. *The White Lyon Inn Yard.*

[*Bar bell rings*] *A Crowd of People some with Port-mantua etc going Across the Stage.*

SERVANT [*at a window*]: Here Waiter! why don't you bring the hot rolls to the Julius Caesar?

1st WAITER: Coming Sir!—hot rolls to the Julius Caesar.

Enter 3 LADIES   [*bar bell rings.*]

What do you want ladies?

1st LADY [*Whispers the Waiter*]: Pray is Cap^n. Patrick O'Shoulder here?

WAITER: He is Ladies—here Will, shew these Ladies into Harry the 8th.   [(*Bar bell rings*) *Ex.* LADIES]

FRIBBLE [*at a window*]: Waiter! will ye, or will ye not bring the Refreshment I order'd an hour ago?

1st WAITER: Coming Sir! coming Sir!

FRIBBLE: You're always a coming, and never stir a Step —the Lady and I are almost perish'd—Waiter—let me have half a dozen more Jellies.   [*Exit.*]

1st WAITER: I shall, Sir—do Tom carry half a dozen Jellies to that Fribbling Gentleman; and the Tall lady in *Love's labour lost*.   [*Bar bell rings.*]

[*Enter* GENTLEMAN *in Slippers.*]

Ostler! Bootcatcher!—where are these fellows? I can get no body near me.—Damn the Jubilee, I can neither eat, or drink or Sleep here—nor get my boots to go somewhere else—why Bootcatcher you Sirrah! where are my boots?

[*Enter Bootcatcher*]

I wish I could tell you, Sir, but you mun do as the rest on 'em—the boots are all thrown together in a heap yonder, and first come, first sarv'd.

1st GENT^n: Zounds mine's a new pair, made a purpose for the Jubilee, and never worn before—I would not lose them for all the Jubilees and Shakespears——   [*runs off.*]

BOOT CATCHER: You need not run so fast Measter, for all the new boots ha' been gone this half hour.

[Bar Bell rings]
[Ex. Bootcatcher.]

Enter 2ND GENT.: I shall be too late for the Pageant—where's my breakfast Waiter?——

[Enter 2d Waiter with Breakfast.]

2ND WAITER: Here, Sir.

2D GENT.: Bring it this way then.   *[Ex. 2D GENT.]*

Enter 3D GENT *[meeting the Breakfast]*: This is my breakfast, where are you carrying it?

2D WAITER: To the other Gentleman.

3D GENT.: One is as good as Another—there's for you *[gives him Money]*—he's a Book Customer—ready money is always serv'd first.   *[Ex. with breakfast.]*
[Bar bell rings]

Ex. WAITER crys: Coming up Sir!

Enter 4TH & 5TH GENT. *[running with some ribs of beef]*: I have got something at last—Come along this is better than starving.   *[Ex. with the Beef.]*

Enter FAT COOK *[running after him]*: Here you with the three ribs of beef!—don't touch 'em,! they are for my Lord's Servants, and they must be serv'd first—See, see, hunger has no manners—they are at it already—what shall I do?—here boy!—Roger!

Enter ROGER: What mun ye ha measter, look I'm ready to do any thing for you, so I am.

COOK: Hold your tongue then.

[79]

Boy: I'll do any thing for you measter, Indeed I will.

Cook: Hold your tongue then you dog and hear what I have to say—[*strikes him*] run to the Butcher's as fast as you can, bid him send me all he has, fat and lean, fresh or not fresh, and bid him kill away—or I must run away.

[*Ex.* Cook & boy *Severally.*]
[*Bar bell rings*]

Irishman: Faith and troth I never complain of want of Sleep whilst I am drinking—but to have no Sleep and no drink, is a little too much upon the Jubilee rig.

Waiter [*at the Window*]: Here where are you all, John, Tom, Harry!

I. Man: Hollo! fait here is a fine hurry, and boddering, and confusion—There's no pleasure at all like a Jubilee— the delight is to be wanting every thing, and get nothing— to see every body busy, and not know what they're about.

Waiter [*at the Window*]: John, Tom, Harry!

I. Man: Hey dey, what's the matter now?

Enter Waiter: Where's my master? call him John—— there's the Devil to do, the Gentleman and ladies are quarrelling again in the *Catherine and Petruchio.* [*Ex.* Waiter]

I. Man: O Let 'em alone — they know what they are about,—it is some of the Married Gentry from the Playhouse, it is a family business, and must be settled by themselves—the only way to make peace is to let them fight it out.

Enter Fellow [*with a box of wooden ware etc.*]: Tooth pick cases, needle cases, punch ladles, Tobacco Stoppers,

Ink-stands, nutmeg Graters, and all sorts of boxes, made
out of the famous Mulberry tree.

I. Man: Here you Mulberry tree,—let me have some of
the true Dandy, to carry back to my wife and Relations in
Ireland.   [*looks at the ware*]

Enter 2d Man [*with ware*]: Don't buy of that fellow
your honour, he never had an Inch of the Mulberry tree
in his life, his Goods are made out of old Chairs and Stools
and colour'd to cheat Gentlefolks with — It was I your
honour bought all the true Mulberry tree, here's my Affi-
davit of it.

1st Man: Yes, you villain, but you sold it all two years
ago, and you have purchas'd since more Mulberry trees
than would serve to hang your whole Generation upon—
he has got a little money your honour, and so nobody must
turn a penny, or cheat Gentlefolks but himself—I wonder
you an't asham'd Robin—do, your honour, take this punch
Ladle.

I. Man: I'll tell you what you Mulberry Scoundrels you, if
you don't clear the Yard of yourselves this minute, and let
me see you out of my sight, you Thieves of the world, my
Oak plant shall be about your Trinkets, and make the Mulberry Juice run down your rogue-Pates — Get away you
Spalpeens you. [*beats 'em off*]

Re Enter Irishman *immediately*: a parcel of Rascals!
want to impose upon a Gentleman that has travell'd in all
the Forreign parts both at home & abroad—They may talk
as they will of their Mulberry Bushes but commend me to
a bit of old Shellalee.

[*Enter a* MAN *beating a Drum,* and Another *leading a large Bin with a Crowd following.*]

The Notified Porcupine Man, and all sorts of outlandish birds, and other strange Beasts to be seen without loss of time on the great Meadow near the Ampi-Theatre at so small a price as one Shilling a piece. Alive, alive, alive, ho!
[*Exit, beats the Drum etc.*]

I. MAN: This foolish fellow won't make his fortune at the Jubilee; to ax a Tirteen to see strange Animals in a house, when one may see 'em for nothing going along the streets, alive, alive, ho!

[*Enter* TRUMPETER *blowing the Trumpet &* MR. & MRS. SAMSON, *& a Crowd of People. They give away Bills etc*]

TRUMPETER: Ladies and Gentlemen—The famous Samson is just going to begin—Just going to mount four horses at once with his feet upon two Saddles—also the most wonderfull Surprizing feats of Horsemanship by the most *Notorious* Mrs Sampson. [*Exeunt blowing the Trumpet*]

IRISHMAN: I warrant her, she rides astride, Honey, wt a Pommel as they do in Ireland. This is a new way of riding upon one's feet—Tho' fait and trot, many a Good Gentleman rides upon his feet from Ireland, and Scotland too. [*Enter* WAITER]: Harkee young fellow here's tree tirteens for you. let me have a bowl of hot punch and a little something to ate in any snug little corner, and here's another tirteen for yourself.

WAITER: Follow me, Sir, and I'll take care of you—I'll take care of you upon my honour, Sir. [*Exit.*]

[82]

I. MAN: Upon my Soul, there is nothing to be done at the
Jubilee, nor no where else fait, without a little bribery and
Corruption — Upon my Conscience I am very Cold with
going to bed in the Post-chaise, so I'll warm myself with a
little hot punch and steal a Nap for nothing into the bargain to refresh me for their Pageant and Fringes and the
rest of their Jubilee.   [*Ex.* IRISHMAN.]

[*Enter* BANNISTER & VERNON *& a number of men, boys
etc.* Mr. VERNON *with the Mulberry Cup in his hand
& fuddled.*]

VERNON: Hollo! boys! don't let us selfishly and niggardly
confine our Joys to ourselves—but let every Jubilee Soul
partake of our Mirth, and our Liquor, at least kiss the cup
and be happy.

BANNISTER: With all my heart, my boy—we have fuddled
ourselves in the house, and now we'll sober ourselves in the
open Air—Let us take t'other taste of the dear Mulberry
Juice.

BANNISTER SINGS:

I

Behold this fair Goblet, 'twas carv'd from the tree,
Which, O my sweet Shakespear, was planted by thee;
As a Relick I kiss it, and bow at the Shrine,
What comes from thy hand must be ever divine!
      All shall yield to the Mulberry tree,
      Bend to thee,
      Blest Mulberry,
      Matchless was he,
      Who Planted thee,
      And thou like him Immortal be!

[83]

VERNON:

The Fame of the Patron gives fame to the tree,
From him and his Merits this takes its degree;
Let Phœbus and Bacchus their Glories resign,
Our Tree shall surpass both the Laurel and Vine.
      All shall yield to the Mulberry tree etc,

2

Ye Trees of the Forest, so rampant & high,
Who spread round their Branches whose heads sweep
    the Sky
Ye Curious Exotics, whom Taste has brought here,
To root out the Natives at prices so dear.
      All shall yield to the Mulberry Tree etc,

3

The Oak is held Royal, is Britains great Boast
Preserv'd once our King, & will always our Coast,
But of Fir we make Ships, we have Thousands that fight;
But where is there one like our Shakespeare can write.
      All shall yield to the Mulberry Tree etc,

4

Let Venus delight in her Gay Myrtle Bowers,
Pomona in Fruit trees, and Flora in Flowers;
The Garden of Shakespeare all fancies will suit,
With the Sweetest of Flowers, & fairest of Fruit.
      All shall yield to the Mulberry Tree etc,

5.

With Learning & Knowledge, the Well Letter'd Birch,
Supplies Law & Physick, and Grace for the Church,
But Law & the Gospel in Shakespeare we find
And he gives the best Physick for Body & Mind.
      All shall yield to the Mulberry Tree etc.

6

The Fame of the Patron gives Fame to the Tree
From him, & his Merits, this takes its degree,
Let Phœbus & Bacchus their Glories resign
Our Tree shall Surpass both the Laurel & Vine.
       All shall yield to the Mulberry Tree etc.

KEAR:

7

The Genius of Shakespear outshines the bright day,
More rapture than wine to the heart can convey,
So the tree which he planted, by making his own,
Has Laurel, and bays, and the Vine all in one.
       All shall yield to the Mulberry tree, etc.

VERNON:

8

Then each take a relick of this hallow'd tree,
From Folly and fashion a charm let it be;
Fill, fill to the planter, the Cup to the brim,
To honour your Country, do honour to him.
       All shall yield to the Mulberry tree,
       Bend to thee,
       Blest Mulberry,
       Matchless was he
       Who Planted thee,
       And thou like him Immortal be!

Drums, fifes, & bells ring.
They all Ex. in a hurry going to see the Pageant.

HERE FOLLOWS THE PAGEANT

*With Bells ringing, fifes playg, drums beating,
& Cannon firing.*

Order of the Pageant in the Jubilee.

All Enter from the Top of the Stage.

9 Men Dancers with Tambourines

3 Graces

9 Women Dancers—Muses

[*They dance down the Stage to Music.*]

2 Men drest in Old English with Mottos of the Theatre *upon rich Standards wᵗʰ proper decorations.*

2 fifes

&

2 Drums;

As You Like It.

Shepherd with a banner

Touchstone ⎱
Audrey   ⎰

Rosalind in boys Cloaths with a Crook ⎱
Orlando   ⎰

Duke Senʳ.—with a Spear.

4 Forresters with spears two and two.

Jaques with a Spear, Melancholly.

Tempest

Sailor with a banner

Ariel with a Wand—raising a Tempest.

A Ship in distress sailing down the Stage—

Prospero with a Wand ⎱
Miranda   ⎰

[86]

Caliban with a wooden bottle & ⎫
2 Sailors all drunk   ⎬

Mercht of Venice

Lancelot with a banner——
2 Men with the Caskets in a rich
Bassanio ⎫
Portia   ⎬
Shylock with a knife, and bond & Scales.

Much Ado etc

Town Clerk with Banner
Benedick & Beatrice in Masquerade.

Two Gentn of Verona

Man with the Banner
The Two Gentlemen of Verona
Launce with his Dog Crab.

Twelfth Night

Clown a banner——
Sir Andw. Aguecheek ⎫
Sir Toby Belch   ⎬ fuddled.
Malvolio with a letter &
his Stockings cross Garter'd.

Midsummer Night's Dream

Bottom with asses head and banner
16 Fairies with banners
Chariot drawn by Butterflies
King & Queen of the Fairies in the Chariot.

Merry Wives of Windsor

Nym with a banner.

Justice Shallow ⎫
Sir Hugh ⎬
Host ⎭

Dr. Caius ⎫
Mrs Quickly ⎬
Rugby ⎭

Slender
Bardolph with a Cup.

M⁀rs. Ford ⎫
Falstaff ⎬ on Horseback
M⁀rs. Page ⎭

Page with Sword & Shield
Pistol
Mouldy
Bullcalf
Wart
Feeble
Shadow.
Venus & Cupid.
The Comic Muse in a Chariot drawn by 5 Satyrs attended by 6 Loves with large antique masks.
All the Chorus (6 Boys & 20 Men dress'd in a Uniform like Arcadian Shepherds) Two & two singing.

Chorus for the Pageant. by Bickerstaff.

Hence ye prophane! and only they,
Our Pageant grace our pomp survey,
Whom love of Sacred Genius brings;
Let Pride, let flattery decree,
Honors to deck the Memory,

[88]

Of Warriors, Senators, and Kings—
Nor less in Glory, and desert,
The Poet here receives his part,
A Tribute from the feeling heart.

3 Graces.

Apollo with his Lyre.

The Statue of Shakespear supported by ye Passions and Surrounded by the seven Muses with their Trophies.

The Kettle drum drawn in a Carr

6 Trumpets—

King Rich^d 3rd

Old Eng: Gent—with a banner——

6 Old English Soldiers with Spears, two & two

King Richard with a Ring——

Tyrrell

Queen leading Prince Edward and the Duke of York.

Richmond with a Truncheon.

Cymbeline

Old Eng: Gent with a banner

Bellarious with a Spear

Arviragus & Guyderius with Spears leading Imogen

Posthumus a Sword & Shield.

Hamlet

Gent^n.—with a banner

Ghost with a Truncheon

Hamlet }
Queen } in ye Closet Scene follows ye Ghost in horror

Ophelia mad with Straw etc

2 Gravediggers. a Pick ax & Spade.

Othello

Soldier—a banner
2 Senators.
Duke — — — — — — }
Brabantio in a Night Gown }

Othello — }
Desdemona }
Iago — — }
Roderigo }

Romeo & Juliet

A Gentleman with a banner.
Peter with a fan — — — }
Nurse with a Crutch stick }

Romeo }
Fryar }
Juliet }
Apothecary.

King Henry 5th

Old Eng^h. Gent. with a banner
2 Old Eng^h Soldiers
2 —— — D^o ——
King Henry 5th
Fluellen with a Leek } Flu: makes Pistol cut ye Leek.
Pistol —— — }

King Lear

Old English Gent^n.—a banner——
Edgar in the mad dress with a Staff—

King Lear }
Kent } Thunder & Lightn^g
Cordelia }

[90]

King Henry 8th

Old Eng: Gent with a banner—
2 Old Eng: Gents.
2 Beef Eaters.
Wolsey }
K: Henry }
Bishop Cranmer }
Q. Catherine— }
4 Beef Eaters

Macbeth

Gent^n. with a banner
Macbeth— }
La: Macbeth }

    Caldron drawn by 4 Dæmons, the Cauldron burning—Hecate & 3 Witches following the Caldron.

Julius Caesar

a Roman Gent^n. with a banner.
6 Romans with Lictors.
Julius Caesar.
Roman Gent with the Eagle.
Soothsayer.
6 Romans with Trophies
Brutus }
Cassius }

Antony & Cleopatra

Sold^r. with a banner in a Persian dress
4 persian Guards with Spears
4 blacks
2 black boys with fans of Peacock feathers fanning=

[91]

= Antony
     &
Cleopatra

2 blacks with Umbrellas
2 black boys to hold up Cleopatra's train
4 Eunuchs
Minerva—
Demon of Revenge with a burning Torch—
The Tragic Muse drawn in a Chariot by
6 Furies—and attended by
Fame
Grief
Pity
Despair
Madness
3 Furies following the Chariot.
Mars
6 Soldiers with Swords & Shields
9 Soldiers with Spears.

The Bells ring 'em off & the Scene changes to a
Street in Stratford

End of the first part

[92]

SECOND PART

SCENE *a Street. in Stratford*

Enter SUKEY *and* NANCY.

SUKEY: There was a sight for you! there was a Pagan!—
If I had not a Shakespur ribbon to pin upon my heart, I
could not have shewn my face—the dear creature is nearest
my heart—I doat upon Shakespur.

NANCY: Law, Cousin Sue, how you talk to a body — I
swear I know no more about the Jubillo, and Shakespur as
you call him, than I do about the Pope of Rome.

SUKEY: Nancy, you have not been out of this poor hole of
a Town, or you would not have such low vulgar fancies in
your head — had you liv'd at Birmingham or Coventry,
or any other polite Cities as I have done, you would have
known better than to talk so, of Shakespur and the Jew-
bill——

NANCY: Why who is this Shakespur, that they make such
a rout about 'en—he was not a Lord?

SUKEY: Lord help you Cousin—he is worth fifty Lords.
why he could write—He cou'd write finely your plays and
your Tragedies; and make your heart leap, or sink in your
bosom, as he pleas'd, 'twas a wonder of a man! I'm sure
I cry'd for a whole night together after hearing his Romy
and July at Birmingham, by the London Gentlemen and
Ladies player people—I never let Mr Robin keep me Company till I had been mov'd by that fine piece: Why he cuts
Romeo into little Stars as fine as fipence. O, the Sweet
Creature—the dear Willy Shakespur.

[93]

The Pride of all nature was sweet Willy O,
    The first of all Swains,
    He Gladden'd the plains,
None ever was like to the sweet Willy O.

2.

He sung it so rarely did sweet Willy O,
    He melted each maid,
    So skilful he play'd,
No Shepherd e'er pip'd like the Sweet Willy O.

3.

He wou'd be a Soldier, the Sweet Willy O,
    When arm'd in the field,
    With Sword and with Shield,
The Laurel was worn by the Sweet Willy O.

4.

He charm'd 'em when living the Sweet Willy O,
    And when Willy dy'd,
    'Twas Nature that sigh'd,
To part with her all in her sweet Willy O.

NANCY: I know nothing of what you talk about not I—but I can't think all this Crowding, trumpetting, Drumming, eating, drinking, ringing, Cannon firing and all this Mummery would be for a poor poet, that liv'd, I don't know how many hundred years ago—I canno' believe what you tell me.

    All this for a Poet—o no,
    Who liv'd Lord knows how long ago?
        How can you Jeer one,
        How can you fleer one,
    A Poet, a poet,—O no,

[94]

'Tis not so,
Who liv'd Lord knows how long ago:

2ᵈ.

It must be some great man,
A Prince, or a State-man,
It cant be a Poet—o no:
        Your poet is poor,
        And Nobody sure,
Regards a poor poet I trow:
        The rich ones we prize,
        Send 'em up to the skies,
But not a poor poet—O no——
Who liv'd Lord knows how long ago.

SUKEY: If you are so vulgar Cousin Nancy—I vow you
shan't go along with me to the Ample-Theatre—don't you
remember the Verses Parson Shrimp wrote upon him.

        If he saw ye he knew ye,
        Would look thro' and thro' ye,
                Thro' skin, and your flesh and your Cloaths,
        Had you Vanity, pride,
        Fifty Follies beside,
                He wou'd see 'em, as plain as your nose.

NANCY:

        Tho' sins I have none,
        I am Glad he is gone,
No Maid wou'd live near such a Mon
        Duet by SUKEY *and* NANCY.
        Let us sing it, and dance it,
        Rejoice it, and prance it,
                That no man has now such an Art;

[95]

What wou'd come of us all,
Both the great ones, and small,
    Should he now live to peep in each heart.
    Tho' sins I have none,
    I am Glad he is gone,
No maid cou'd live near such a Mon.

                    [Exeunt Singing & Dancing]

Enter IRISHMAN. [*Drunk*]: Hollo! you sweet Jubilee wenches, come here you dear craturs, Stand still and see who you are running away from you little precious Devils. —here's Old Ireland for you, you dear Craturs I'll follow you, you dear little Jewels, I will.   [*Exit.*]

        SCENE, *a Landskip.*
        Re-enter IRISHMAN

Where are you—you dear precious craturs—I'll find you out after your Pageant fringes are gone by.

      Enter ROGER *& Crosses ye Stage.*

IRISHMAN: Here you boy with the Strait Colour'd head of hair.

BOY: What would you have Master make haste for I'm in a wounded hurry.

I. MAN: When will the Pageant fringes be after coming by here?

ROGER: La! Sir, the Pagans are all gone by already! and now they are all crowding like mad folks into the great round house on the Meadow—and I'm going there too—Your Servant—I mun go—I munno lose the fine sight—Your Servant. The Pagans are all gone by. [*Exit rung.*]

I. MAN: O this is fine usage faith! after coming all the

[96]

way from Ireland to see the Shakespear fringes and Pageant, and them thieves of the world, them waiters, to let a Gentleman Sleep all the while it was going past, because they knew very well, I could not see it if I was not awake [*Rain behind*] Och hone!—it does not rain to be sure—'tis a fine affair to bring Gentlemen out in such weather—this would not be suffer'd in Dublin, without calling this fellow of a Steward to an Account—I shall give a fine account of my travels—I came here three hundred Miles to lie in a Post-Chaise without Sleep, and to Sleep when I shou'd be awake, to get nothing to ate, and pay double for that—and now I must return back in the rain, as great a fool as those who hate to stay in their own Country, and return from their travels as much Improv'd as I myself shall when I go back to Kilkenny—However I'll try & get into some Corner of yᵉ Round House too—& if I can't get in, Ara! I'll go home & be nowhere.   [*Exit.*]

Garrick's *The Jubilee*. Garrick's stage direction for the last scene. From the MS. in the Henry E. Huntington Library.

Last Scene

Is a magnificent transparent one—in which the Capital Characters of Shakespeare are exhibited at full length—with Shakespeare's Statue in ye Middle crown'd by Tragedy & Comedy, fairies & Cupids surrounding him, & all the Banners waving at ye Upper End. then Enter the Dancers, and then the Tragic & Comic Troops—and range themselves in the Scene.

Chorus from the first Entrance Singing.

This is the day, a holiday! a holiday!
Drive Spleen and rancour far away,
This is the day, a holiday! a holiday!
Drive care and sorrow far away.
Here Nature nurs'd her Darling Boy
From whom all Care & Sorrow fly
    Whose Harp the Muses Strung;
From heart to heart let Joy rebound,
Now, now, we tread Enchanted Ground
    Here Shakespeare walk'd & Sung.

A Dance of the Graces—Muses etc.

After the Dance they all come forward and Sing the following Roundelay.

MRS. BADDELEY *as Venus:*

    Sisters of the tuneful strain!
    Attend your Parents Jocund train,
    'Tis fancy calls you, follow me
        To Celebrate the Jubilee.

[101]

MR. VERNON 2 *as Apollo:*

> On Avon's banks, where Shakespear's bust,
> Points out, and Guards his Sleeping dust,
> The Sons of Scenic Mirth decree
> > To Celebrate this Jubilee.

MISS RADLEY 3 *as a Muse:*

> Come, daughters, come, and bring with you
> Th' Aerial Sprites and Fairy crew,
> And the Sister Graces three,
> > To Celebrate our Jubilee.

MR. VERNON 4:

> Hang around the Sculptur'd tomb
> The broider'd vest, the nodding plume,
> And the Mask of Comic Glee,
> > To Celebrate our Jubilee.

MR. BANNISTER 5 *as Comus:*

> From Birnam Wood, and Bosworth's field,
> Bring the Standard, bring the Shield,
> With Drums, and Martial Symphony,
> > To Celebrate our Jubilee.

MRS. BADDELEY 6:

> In Mournful Numbers now relate
> Poor Desdemona's hapless fate,
> With frantic deeds of Jealousy,
> > To Celebrate our Jubilee.

MISS RADLEY 7:

> Nor be Windsor's Wives forgot,
> With their harmless merry plot,
> The Whit'ning Mead, and haunted tree,
> > To Celebrate our Jubilee.

MR. BANNISTER 8:

> Now in Jocund strains recite,
> The Revels of the braggar'd Knight,
> Fat Knight! and Antient Pistol he!
> To Celebrate our Jubilee.

MR. VERNON 9:

> But see in Crowds, the Gay, the fair,
> To the Splendid Scene repair,
> A Scene as fine, as fine can be,
> To Celebrate our Jubilee.

Every Character tragic & Comic Join in the Chorus and go back during which the Guns fire, bells ring etc. etc. and the Audience applaud.

Bravo Jubilee!

Shakespeare for Ever!

The End

NOTES

THE JUBILEE

The Jubilee. The Shakespearean Club of Stratford-upon-Avon, which was founded at the Falcon Inn on the 23rd of April, 1824, formed with the purpose of organizing every third year a celebration similar to that which Garrick instituted at Stratford in the early days of September, 1769. Hence, three years after the establishment of this club, on the 23rd of April, 1827, this Shakespearean Club organized a Jubilee celebration at Stratford, (the first of its kind since Garrick's) which began on the poet's birthday and continued for the next two days. Garrick's program was followed precisely. There were cannon-firing, fire-works, Ode-recitation, a procession of Shakespearean characters, breakfasts, dinners, and the laying of the cornerstone of the new theatre. This ceremony was performed by the Mayor of the Borough, Mr. John Mills. In 1872, this first theatre was demolished, and in 1877, the first stone of the present Shakespeare Memorial Theatre was laid.

On the poet's birthday of 1830, the second Jubilee celebration after Garrick's began and lasted for three days. On the first day, Charles Kean played Sir Giles Overreach in Massinger's *New Way to Pay Old Debts;* on April 24th, Richard III; and on the last night of the celebration, he acted another Shakespearean character.

Garrick's *The Jubilee.* On the title page of this play appears a memorandum, written by Garrick, of some books that he lent to Dr. Burney on October 5, 1771. Following this we find a note by Kemble which reads:

The Jubilee.

Written by David Garrick Esq[r].

The Manuscript Notes, as well as the Memoranda at the top of this Page, are in M^r. Garrick's Handwriting—J.P.K. Collated & Perfect. J. P. K. 1800

PAGE 71. *round house*. This has reference to the amphitheatre built on the banks of the Avon for the Jubilee. Almost all the activities connected with the Jubilee took place in this structure.

PAGE 71. *Shew People and Shakespeare's Image*. Shakespeare's bust in the church at Stratford-upon-Avon had probably received a fresh coat of paint in honor of the Jubilee.

"In the year 1748, this monument was carefully repaired, and the original colors of the bust, etc as much as possible preserved, (by Mr. John Hall, a limner of Stratford,) by receipts arising from the performance of the play of Othello, at the old Town-hall, on Tuesday, the 9th day of September, 1746; and generously given by Mr. John Ward, (grand-father of the present Mrs. Siddons,) manager of a company of comedians then performing in the town; and in 1793, the bust and figures above it, . . . , were painted white, . . . to suit the present taste."— *History and Antiquities of Stratford-upon-Avon*, by R. B. Wheeler. Stratford-upon-Avon, [1806], pp. 73–75.

PAGES 71–72. *Steward*. This is a description of Garrick as the Steward of the Jubilee.

PAGE 74. *The Jubilee*. The following passage was Garrick's original account of the Jubilee.

MUSICIAN (*imitating Foote*): I'll tell you, Sir; This is what Foote said of ye Jubilee in his Devil upon two Sticks.

[108]

a Jubilee is to invite the people of England to go a hundred miles post without horses — to a Borough without Representatives—Govern'd by a Mayor and Aldermen who are no Magistrates. There, in a Crowd without Company, you'll find Music without Melody, Odes without Poetry, Dinners without Victuals, and Lodgings without beds.

For some reason or other, probably to avoid trouble, Garrick omitted Foote's account of the Jubilee and inserted one of his own composition.

PAGE 75. *Great big Inn.* The White Lion Inn.

PAGE 75. *all the plays writ upon the doors.* The rooms in the White Lion Inn are not numbered but named after Shakespeare's plays.

PAGE 75. *Mulberry box upon his breast.* This has reference to the mulberry medallion engraved with the likeness of Shakespeare and richly set in gold which, throughout the festivities, Garrick wore suspended from a ribbon about his neck.

PAGE 76. *Vernon* and *Dibdin.* Members of Garrick's company.

PAGE 77. *Scene* 3rd. Garrick's note to this stage direction (on the opposite page) reads:

[N. B. this is perhaps a Scene of ye most regular confusion that was Ever exhibited.]

PAGE 83. *Pageant and Fringes.* Pageant has reference to the procession of Shakespearean characters. Garrick explains the word "Fringes" in his working copy of this play *The Jubilee* (in the Barton-Ticknor Collection of the Boston Public Library) as "franchises."

THREE PLAYS BY DAVID GARRICK

PAGE 83. *Bannister*. Another of Garrick's actors.

PAGE 83. *Behold this fair Goblet*. This is Garrick's mulberry cup (carved from the wood of Shakespeare's mulberry tree) which was presented to Garrick by the Mayor and the Corporation of Stratford at the time of the Jubilee celebration. It was elaborately carved, with a cover surmounted by a branch of mulberry leaves and fruit, the whole standing on a base of silver. It was sold at Christie's on May 5, 1825.

PAGE 84. *The Fame of the Patron*. On the page opposite this stanza appears the following note:

Shd this Stanza be repeated twice? Better as Stanza 6.

It appears again as stanza six.

PAGE 86. *Order of the Pageant etc*. Garrick's note to this stage direction (on the opposite page) reads:

[*N. B.* in the procession Every Scene in ye different Plays represents some capital part of it in Action.]

PAGE 87. *Midsummer Night's Dream*. The note to this section of the pageant is as follows:

Suppose Bottom & Q of Fs asleep in ye Chariot—& K. of F—drops her Eyes with ye Flower, turns out Bottom & takes his Place & She awakes etc.

PAGE 87. *Merry Wives*. A note at this point, not in Garrick's hand, reads thus:

What is ye whim of having These particularly on Horseback? Cathe & Petruchio with ye lame dismal Horse & all P's miserable Geer, as describ'd by Grumio, wd have had a fine Effect. I wd introduce C & P. in this Manner & four Fellows shd bring in Sr John in ye Buck Basket, ye Wives on either Side covering him with foul Cloaths, & he endeavouring to get out.

PAGE 88. *Bickerstaff.* The chorus for the pageant was written by Isaac Bickerstaff (1735–c. 1812). He was the author of a large number of plays.

PAGE 93. *Shakespur ribbon.* Ribbons of variegated hues worn by the visitors at the Jubilee celebration to illustrate the line

"Each change of many-color'd life he drew,"
from Johnson's prologue which was written for the opening of the Drury Lane Theatre on September 15, 1747.

PAGE 96. *Pagans.* Pageant.

PAGE 97. (*Rain behind*). This stage direction refers to the rain which frustrated the exhibition of the pageant of Shakespearean characters at the Stratford Jubilee.

PAGE 101. *Mrs. Baddeley* was one of the prominent women members of Garrick's company. She was the original Fanny Sterling in Garrick and Colman's *The Clandestine Marriage.*

THE MEETING OF
THE COMPANY

or

BAYES'S ART OF ACTING

INTRODUCTION

GARRICK'S prelude, *The Meeting of the Company or Bayes's Art of Acting*, produced on September 17, 1774,[1] ushered the 1774–75 season into the Drury Lane Theatre. This little piece is a descendant of a long and distinguished line of satires, and resembles closely its famous ancestor, *The Rehearsal*,[2] which was written by George Villiers, Second Duke of Buckingham, with the assistance of Martin Clifford and Thomas Sprat, and to which, it is said, Samuel Butler of Hudibrastic fame also contributed. *The Rehearsal* was originally intended as a satire against Davenant; but after Sir William's death, the ridicule was directed against Sir Robert Howard, Dryden's brother-in-law, and finally against Dryden himself. Although the Bayes of Buckingham's play resembles Dryden to a great extent, the character also bears some resemblance to its originals, Davenant and Sir Robert Howard.

The play within a play as a means of satire was a favorite method with dramatists. It was used with excellent results by Beaumont in his *Knight of the Burning Pestle*, in which the Elizabethan dramatist satirizes, in Don Quixotic fashion, the romances of chivalry and the bourgeois drama of his day. Taking the framework of Beaumont's play as his model, Buckingham built his admirable burlesque, *The Rehearsal*, which, in its turn, served as the pattern for the

---

[1] Genest, V, 440.

[2] *The Rehearsal* was produced at the Theatre Royal on December 7, 1671. (Genest, I, 112.)

plays of Fielding, Foote, Garrick, and finally for perhaps the most brilliant of all, Sheridan's *The Critic*.

In both Buckingham's and Garrick's plays, we find the same type of hero, namely, the foolishly solemn, coxcomical, and opinionated poet Bayes. The Bayes of Garrick's piece, however, is painted in miniature. While the Bayes of Buckingham's play sets out to manufacture plots and turn verse into prose and prose into verse, according to the rules in his book, *Drama Commonplaces*, Garrick's hero, with his book, *Bayes's Art of Acting etc.*, in his hand, undertakes to remould actors, "making the worst equal to the best" and "turning tragedians into Comedians and vice versa." Upon the aims of these vainglorious heroes, hinges the satire of both the Restoration and Eighteenth Century burlesques. Incidentally, however, both dramatists hold up to ridicule the reigning absurdities of the theatre of their day.

Garrick's little play gives an excellent picture of some of the doings behind the stage of the Drury Lane Theatre of 1774. The preparations for the rehearsal for the opening performance of the season; the manager's woes; the peevishness of some of the players; the conceit of others; the pompousness and self-complacency of the dramatist; and finally the rehearsal itself, are all admirably well presented.

The piece is prefaced by a petition to the Lord Chamberlain, in which Garrick requests that official's consent to the production of the play. After Garrick's signature, the words "for M^r. Lacy & himself" are added.[3]

---

[3] This is Willoughby Lacy, who, on the death of his father, James Lacy, in January, 1774, became co-manager with Garrick of the Drury Lane Theatre.

Garrick entrusted this play to a notable cast including such actors as King, Weston, and Parsons. King most probably took the part of Bayes. Knight, in his article on Weston in the *Dictionary of National Biography*,[4] says that Weston personated Thomas King in this playlet. This statement, however, is incorrect. As will be seen after reading Garrick's burlesque, Thomas King as himself does not appear but is merely referred to. Weston interpreted his own droll self, while Parsons appeared for Parsons.

The Meeting of the Company was well received. Genest states that it was acted about ten times.[5]

[4] *Dictionary of National Biography*, LX, 376.
[5] Genest, V, 440.

THE MEETING OF
THE COMPANY

or

BAYES'S ART OF ACTING

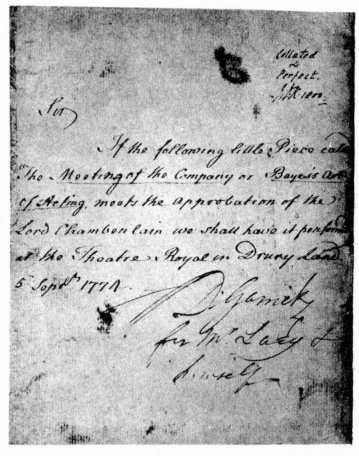

Garrick's petition to the Lord Chamberlain for permission to produce *The Meeting of the Company or Bayes's Art of Acting.* From the MS. in the Henry E. Huntington Library.

Sir.

If the following little Piece call'd *The Meeting of the Company* or *Bayes's Art of Acting*, meets the Approbation of the Lord Chamberlain we shall have it perform'd at the Theatre Royal in Drury Lane 5 Septr 1774.

D. GARRICK
for M^r. Lacy & himself.

The Curtain rises & discovers the Stage full of different people at Work. Painters, Gilders, Carpenters etc. Singers —Singing, Dancers dancing—Actors & Actresses Saluting each other, & all seem busy.

Enter PHILL [*the Carpenter*] : Upon my word Gentlemen & Ladies, if you won't clear the Stage, we can never be ready to open the House to-morrow.

Enter PROMPTER: What's the matter Phill, always a Scolding.

PHILL: We shall never be ready if you don't give up the Stage to us! Lower the Clouds there Rag, and bid Jack Trundle sweep out the Thunder Trunk, we had very slovenly Storms last Season. Mr Hopkins did you ever see such a Litter, & hear such a Noise?

PROMPTR: Yes very often—indeed Ladies and Gentlemen. You must practise your Singing & Dancing elsewhere, or we Shan't ever be ready.

BALLET MASTER: Come along then Gentlemen & Ladies we'll go below.   [*Dancing off*]

SINGER: And we'll practise in the Green room.
                                   [*Exit Singing & books*]
PHILL: We shall do pretty well now.—what with Coronations—Installations, Portsmouth Reviews, Masquerades, Jubilees,—Fete Champetres & the Devil—we have no rest at all—Master's head is always at work, & we are never Idle;—If they want the perpetual motion let 'em come to our Theatre—come bustle my Lads—clear away there——
                                                    [*Exit.*]

[125]

Enter PARSONS: How do you Master Prompter?—Lame still I find—You have no Enemy but the Gout.

PROMPT^R: And is not that enough?—I have try'd every thing & nothing will do;—My Body is starv'd with Abstinence, & my pocket pick'd by the Leige Doctor, & this is my Reward. [*shewing his foot*] I am too poor to be made a fool of—My betters can afford it.

PARSONS: Ay, that Leige Doctor undertook for about Ten thousand Pounds, to set a Number of Gouty Folks a Dancing in a Twelve month, but before the time, he danc'd off with the money, & Death danc'd off with him the Year after.

PROMPTER: With the Gout in his Stomach—But what has recover'd *You* so well—If you are as Plump in the Pocket as you are in the face, You have made a good Campaign, & the Country agrees with you.

PARSONS: Pretty well M^r. Hopkins—We set out heavily but we mended our pace — Liv'd very well — paid our Debts, had some bad Houses—some indifferent & many very good ones—a few Quarrels, an Intrigue or two, & Indispositions as usual.

Enter some ACTRESSES

How do you Ladies, You are welcome to Town again [*Salutes them*] Miss Platt the Managers desire you will be ready in this part by to-morrow Night—tis very short, & very easy study.

MISS PLATT: I have been harrass'd all the Summer, & now I must sit up all Night, to Study this dab of a thing—Managers never consider the wear & tear of a Constitution.

[*Exit peevishly.*]

[126]

Enter Weston

Parsons

What little Tom Weston give me your hand boy!

Weston

As tall as yourself goodman Parsons the Giant.

Parsons.

Come, come, we won't dispute about a quarter
of an Inch. — You are a new man, so sleek so
clear, & the end of your Nose as fair, as the rest
of your face — what have you been doing Boy?

Weston

Turn'd over a New leaf.

Parsons

In some Tavern book I suppose.

Weston

No, no, the leaves there were quite full I was
oblig'd to reform having no Money — I am taking
care of my Constitution.

Parsons

Reform! I should be glad to hear what you cale
Reformation.

Weston

Why, what other folks call Reformation
I live soberly when I am ill, in order to get well,
& when I am well, I live a little pleasantly too'

Garrick's _The Meeting of the Company or Bayes's Art of Acting._ From
the MS. in the Henry E. Huntington Library.

PARSONS: Now the old work begins—Jingle Jangle from September to June.

PROMPTER: I shall now get things ready for the Rehearsal.

Enter WESTON   [*Exit*]

PARSONS: What little Tom Weston give me your hand Boy.

WESTON: As tall as yourself goodman Parsons the Giant.

PARSONS: Come, come, we won't dispute about a quarter of an Inch.—You are a New Man, so sleek so clear, & the end of your Nose as fair, as the rest of your face—what have you been doing Boy?

WESTON: Turn'd over a New leaf.

PARSONS: In some Tavern book I suppose.

WESTON: No, no, the leaves there were quite full—I was oblig'd to reform having no Money—I am taking care of my Constitution.

PARSONS: Reform! I should be glad to hear what you call Reformation.

WESTON: Why, what other folks call Reformation. I live Soberly when I am ill, in order to get well, & when I am well, I live a little pleasantly to get ill again. There would be no variety without it.

PARSONS: None of your Variety for me.

WESTON: Besides—*there's a pleasure in being ill which none but Actors know.*

PARSONS: I don't understand you.

WESTON: It vexes a Manager, & pays him in kind—I love to pay my Debts when I am able—but talk of the Manager, & he is here.

[129]

Enter PATENT [*Performers meeting him*]: Gentlemen &
Ladies your Servant—All meet me with Chearful smiling
Faces—what a pity it is, that they should grow Cold &
Cloudy with the Winter. — Mʳ. Parsons your Servant —
Tom Weston your hand—all in Spirits, I hope, & ready to
take the Field.

PARSONS: The Army Catches Spirit from the General. I
rejoice to see You so well—We were damp'd by the News
Papers.

PATENT: Ay, ay, they kill'd me one day & reviv'd me the
next—Newspaper Life, like *real* Life is chequer'd, a Mix-
ture of good & Evil; what they took away Yesterday, they'll
give again to-morrow; sometimes dead, sometimes alive—
Now praise, now blame, make holes & darn 'em again, can
anything be more impartial?

WESTON: What may any Man who gives me a Plaister
have Liberty to break my head?

PATENT: Break your Vanity's head you mean Tom.—If
the Fools of our Profession, would have more Sensibility
upon the Stage, & less off it They might Strut their hour
without fretting—Let 'em never play the Fool but when
they ought to do it—be as fine Gentlemen as they can in
their business, & never assume the Character out of it—&
the Newspapers won't hurt 'em.

PARSONS: But to be always in fear of a Cat o' nine Tails.

PATENT: This Paper Police may go a little too far sometimes, & so will Constables & Justices of the Peace, & therefore would you have none? Come, come, if we and our
betters were not well watch'd, the State and the Stage would

both suffer for it—but Mum—this is only among ourselves
—Now let us prepare for Action.

WESTON: We'll do our best General—Good pay, & well
paid, is the Nerves of War—had I the Salary of a General,
I could Command an Army as well as the best.

[*A Tragedy Actor comes from the rest.*]

With Submission Mr. Weston—what did you mean by say-
ing you could Command an Army?

WESTON: I meant to say, that I could play Tragedy as well
as the best of you.

ALL: ha! ha! ha!

PATENT: Well said Tom—ha! ha! ha!——

WESTON: And I would do it too—*who's afraid?*

TR. ACTR: Don't imagine Sir, because you can make an
Audience laugh in Jerry Sneak, Dr. Last etc that you can
speak Heroic Verse & touch the Passions.   [*struts about*]

WESTON: Why not—I can set my arms so, take two strides,
roar as well as the best of you, & look like an owl.

TR. ACTR: Is there nothing else requisite to form a Tragedian?   [*with contempt*]

WESTON: O yes, the perriwig maker to make me a bush, a
Taylor a hoop petticoat, a carpenter a Truncheon, a Shoe-
maker high heels, & Cork Soles—and as for Strange Faces,
& Strange Noises, I can make them my Self.

PATENT: Pray Gentlemen don't quarrel about Nothing, &
before the Season begins.

TRA. ACTR: About Nothing Mr. Patent?

PATENT: Dear Mr. Hurst, don't put on a Tragedy face to me, Mr. Bayes will be here directly, & he'll prove to us all, that there is nothing in Acting Tragedy or Comedy.

WESTON: He proves there's nothing in writing them?

PATENT: You may Jest if you please—But Mr. Bayes is very Serious.

PARSONS: Not the less foolish for that.

PATENT: As you shall see by his Letter—there read it.

[*gives the Letter*]

WESTON: How do you know that I can—I'll try whether I have not forgot.   [*They get about him while he reads*]

Sir

Tho you & your Players us'd me & my Play very ill—I will See you, & your Players again.

PARSONS: A very good reason that.

WESTON [*reading*]: Tho' you & your Players have depriv'd me of my Just rights & profits, I will never the less be the making of you both.

PATENT: There's a good Christian for you!

WESTON [*reads*]: I have discover'd a method to make the worst Actors equal to the best—As you have plenty to work upon——

PARSONS: We are much oblig'd to him.

WESTON [*reads*]: If you will promise to perform my Play, I will instruct your players directly; As they are a kind of Smoakey Chimnies, I'll undertake 'em—no Cure no pay— Say, ay, or no—Yours if you are wise——

Bayes.

[132]

WESTON: We are Smoaky Chimnies are we?—We shall Smoak him I believe if he comes.

BAYES [*without*]: Pray take my Cloak young Man — & show me to the Manager.

PATENT: Here he comes—Tom don't be too Riotous but listen to him & Learn.

WESTON: Rather too old for that.

Enter BAYES: M^r. Patent, Your humble Servant—Gentlemen & Ladies—I may be your Friend, if you are not your own Enemies;—let all past mistakes be forgotten, & let us begin a new Score.

WESTON: I always do, wherever I can.

BAYES: I hope you have all had a Successful Summer. I dare say you have all fill'd your Pockets the poor people in the Country know no better.

TR. ACT^R: There are very good Judges in Country Towns M^r. Bayes.

BAYES: And you are a very good Actor in a Country Town M^r. Hurst; You roar, & they Clap—'tis all very well—one man's Meat, is another Man's poison—we must all live M^r. Hurst—I wish you Joy of your Country Judges, & your Country Judges Joy of you, with all my heart. What my old Friend M^r. Bransby? I sincerly wish you Joy—I heard of your fame in the Country.

BRANSBY: I have not been in the Country. [*roughly*]

BAYES: I mean M^r.—when you were in the Country.

BRANSBY: I have not been there, for many Years.

BAYES: So much the better—between You & me, You are much in the right on't.

[133]

Enter BADDELEY.

Mr. Baddeley your hand—I regard you as a Brother Author, —your Magic Lanthorn has bewitch'd everybody—what have you produc'd some Ridiculous characters?

BADDELEY: Very Ridiculous indeed!

BAYES: I hope you will lash the bad Poets, ha?

BADDELEY: I have not yet—but in my next Edition I have such a Character of a Poet.

BAYES: I rejoice to hear it;—tell me a little, Is he ridiculous?

BADDELEY: O yes, a conceited old Fool, whose Vanity makes him ridiculous, even to the Lamp Lighters of the Theatre.

BAYES: Good, good—go on—[*Chuckles.*]

BADDELEY: Tho' old, there is not an Infirmity of the mind which he has not; to Crown the whole, with a face as rough as mine, & a Wig like yours, he fancies himself a Beau Garcon, & Gallants the Ladies.

BAYES: What an old Fool it must be!—work him, & Jerk him, I beg of you.   [*both Laugh*]

BADDELEY: Never fear me.

BAYES: But Mr. Baddeley—when you speak of him again don't make any Comparisons between your face & my Wig I beg of you,—take that hint from me. and I wish your performance a continuance of Publick favour.

BADDELEY: Neither your heir or mine, will be much the Richer for our Scribling Mr. Bayes.   [*Exit*]

BAYES: *Scribling—our Scribling!*—how we Apples Swim? —A Word with you Mr. Patent—As I came through the

Hall, there were some of your Actors, to whom I gave a very proper Salute; (careless indeed, but civil) to which they made little or no Return.

PATENT: Indeed!

BAYES: One in particular dress'd in Red, with a cock'd Hat, black beard, & a cane dangling upon his wrist—look'd full in my face & laugh'd at me.

PATENT: It was Tom King—I am sure he meant nothing.

BAYES: I know that very well. I don't expect meaning from them, but Submission & Civility—your Players appear to me rather more conceited than they were;—indeed there was little room for any Addition in that particular.

PATENT: The Matter is this Mr. Bayes—being Just return'd from the Country, where they Play Kings & Heroes, & they can't be lower'd immediately — In a few days by good Discipline & waking them from their dreams of Royalty, they'll be very Civil again, & very good Subjects.

BAYES: Poor Fellows—their weak heads are easily turn'd, but we'll fix 'em. Do you about your Business Mr. Patent, and I'll to mine—When I have giv'n 'em a Lecture or two, you shall hear them.

PATENT: I will prepare Matters for opening the Season, & you for carrying it on Successfully. [*Exit.*]

BAYES: Leave that to me;—If I don't chip your Blocks into some Shape, Say I am no workman. [*pulls out his book*]

WESTON: Are you a Carpenter Mr. Bayes?

BAYES: Figurative Mr. Weston—I am fond of figures & make a good one, whenever I can.

PARSONS: I see you do. [*looking at him from top to toe.*]

BAYES: Gentlemen & Ladies, oblige me with your Attention.—As Musick is said to have Charms *To Sooth the Savage Beast, to soften Rocks, & bend the Knotted Oak.*—I shall convey my Instructions to you in very Musical Numbers; it will indeed be the only way to break thro' & Soften that strong Rocky, knotty Crusty matter which Nature has (as I may say) envelop'd you with; I shall convince the World in this instance as I have in others, that I will always oppose Nature—that I am above her, & dispise her—But to Business—Here is the Grand Specific! Surround me, my good Patients take your Medicines kindly—To ascertain my right to the Invention, & secure my Property, for these are Theivish times—I call it

Bayes's Art of Acting

or

The Worst equal to the Best.

A very comfortable Remedy for you my good Friends,—So take it without loss of time—I will not only make the worst equal to the best, but the Tragedians, Comedians, & Vice Verso.

WESTON: Vice Versy—what's that pray?

BAYES: That is, I will make the Comedians, Tragedians.

WESTON: That's good News Parsons—that Vice Versy—

PARSONS: Who knows but you & I may play Brutus & Cassius.

BAYES: Silence I beseech you—who among you is the Least fit to be either the Hero in Tragedy or fine Gentleman in Comedy? Let him come forward—to shew the force of my art, I will begin with him first—Not a Soul of 'Em will Stir.

WESTON: M^r. Bayes put it the other way—and ask who is most fit for a Hero, & fine Gentleman, & try the Effect of it.

BAYES: Thank you—Any Gentleman (I say) that is most fit for the Characters of a Hero, or fine Gentleman, may begin the Experiment.   [*They all come forward*]

WESTON: I told you so M^r. Bayes—All Hero's & fine Gentlemen!—Now Gentlemen you may go back again—for I'll be the Man—I'm not asham'd to own that I am the least fit.

BAYES: And therefore the most fit—You shall both be a Hero & fine Gentleman, & you won't be the first little Man, who has try'd at both.

ALL: Ha! ha! ha!—Now for it Tom!——

BAYES: Before I begin, I must tell you, that I intend to extend my Scheme to Poetry, Painting, & Musick, & will in a few years make Genius of as little Consequence in this Nation, as a fine Complexion, which you know Ladies is to be bought of any French Milliner in the Bills of Mortality. —Pray be silent, you'll never have such another Opportunity.

[*he reads*]

"Of giving Life to Clods I make profession,
"Grace to the Lame, & to the blind Expression,
"In me the dullest Mortal finds a friend,
"I beg you all for your own sakes attend;
     "Whither your Bias be,
     "To skip & Grin in Comedy,
     "Or Rant & roar in Tragedy,
     "It is all one to me.

[137]

WESTON: That we do verily believe.——

BAYES: When I come to some striking forcible lines, you must all by way of a Greek Chorus, repeat & act them—I wish that some Scholars, & Gentlemen of the University were here, it would give 'em great pleasure.

Shakespeare has said—A Silly Empty Creature!
"Never o'erstep the Modesty of Nature

"I say you *must* to prove it I engage,
"Whate'er your Sex, or Character, or age,
"No Modesty will do upon the Stage.

WESTON: Ladies pray mind what the Gentleman sais to you.

BAYES: And pray mind the following String of Similes if you love good writing.

WESTON: I wish I could return the favour with another String.—— [*aside*]

BAYES:

"Genius a *Gem*, search all the Kingdom round,
"Is not on Ev'ry Dunghill to be found,
"Therefore in Charity I come to tell,
"How *Bristol Stones*, well set will do as well.

PARSONS: Brethern of the Bristol Company, there is some Comfort for us.

BAYES: I'll comfort you all, Man Woman & Child before I have done with you. [*reads*]
"Nature's a Bird, & ev'ry fool will fail
"Who hopes to lay some Salt upon her Tail,
"In vain to Seize the Wanton, Boobies watch her,

[138]

"They've neither Eyes, legs, hands or heads to catch
 her.

Ergo, 'tis not worth your while to run after her.

WESTON: I'll try a little for all that.

BAYES [*reads*]: "Gold is a scarce Commodity——

WESTON: So it is.

BAYES: Don't interrupt me——   [*reads*]

"Gold is a scarce Commodity—but *Brass*,

"Of which no Scarcety, as well may pass.

WESTON: There's Comfort again for us, these hard times—

BAYES: That I may not Burden your minds too much,
which may be overloaded already; I shall comprise the Art
of Acting Comedy & Tragedy in a few lines—You have
heard of the Iliad in a Nut Shell—here it is.

                                   [*shews the paper*]

WESTON: Crack away, & give us the Kernel.

BAYES [*reads*]:

"First Gentlemen, turn Nature out of door,

"Then Rant away, 'till you can rant no more,

"Walk, talk, & look, as none walk'd, talk'd, &
     look'd before.

PARSONS: We can all do that.

WESTON: And have done it, a hundred times.

BAYES: Silence! or you are undone.

WESTON: Mum!

BAYES [*reads*]:

"Would you in Tragedy Extort applause,

"Distort *Yourselves*,—now Rage, now Start—now
     pause,

[139]

"Beat breast, roll Eyes, stretch Nose, up brows,
 down Jaws,

"Then strut, stride, stare, Goggle, bounce, & Bawl,

"And when you're out of breath—pant, drag, &
 drawl.

There's a picture for you Gentlemen & Ladies.

WESTON: And a devellish Ugly one.

BAYES: Repeat it after me & act it.

WESTON: "Wou'd you in Tragedy etc.

BAYES [*reads*]:

 "Be in extremes in Buskin, or in Sock,

 "In action Wild—in attitude a Block!

 "From the Spectator's Eye, your faults to hide,

 "Be either Whirlwind,—or be petrify'd.

Exampli—Gratia—mind Gentlemen & Ladies——
[he reads]

 "I thurst for Vengeance, bring me Fiends, a Cup,

 "Large as my Soul, that I may drink it up.

WESTON: That I may drink it up—that's good.
[licks his lips]

BAYES: But you must not drink it up with Joy, M^r. Weston.

WESTON: I can't help it—You must alter the figure.

BAYES: Not for all the Wine in the Kingdom—mind me.
[he reads]

 " 'Tis only blood can quench me—thus I draw

 "My droughty Dagger—& thus Slake it—ha!
[Starts into an Attitude]

There's Start, pant, pause, drag, & drawl for you! Now
Chorus all. 'Tis only Blood etc.

[140]

They all Chorus

" 'Tis only Blood etc

BAYES: Are you all block'd in Attitude—tell me Somebody for I can't Stir.——

PARSONS [*in an attitude*] : Nor I.——

WESTON: Block & all—Block I assure you M^r. Bayes from one end to the other.

BAYES: Thank ye Gentlemen—But to proceed——

"To heighten Terror—be it wrong or right,

"Be black your Coat, your handkerchief be white,

"Thus pull your hair to add to your distress,

"What your face cannot, let your Wig Express.

I have seen a Romeo so Expeditious, that he has been dress'd like a Bridegroom in one Scene, & in the next Slap he has a compleat Suit of Mourning made & dresses himself in it from top to toe, before the Taylor could finish a single Button hole.   [*he reads*]

"Your Author's words, or lengthen 'em or lop 'Em,

"Stretch 'em in Tragic Scenes—in Comic chop 'em,

"On Tragic rack, first stretch the word & tear—

"Crack Nerves—burst brain, Rivet me Despa-a-re.

Crack Nerves—burst brain—*there's a Tear for you!* Rivet me despa-a-a-air—*& there's a Stretch for you!* Mind & mark all your r'rs too, or you won't outstep the Modesty of Nature.

"Cr'rck—bur'rst—Ner'rves—brain—rivet

        Despa-a-a-air,

I'll make a word of Two Syllables, two & Twenty if I please—I shall reach their hearts one way or another.

WESTON: If you have a Receipt for Men as well as words, I wish you would stretch me, & Parsons a little.

BAYES: You may have your wish sooner than you expect, Gentlemen—tho, I can't make tall Men of You, I'll make great Men of You, which is a better thing.

[*he reads*]

"Observe in Comedy to frisk about,

"Never stand still—Jerk, work—fly in—fly out,
Your faults conceal in flutter, & in hurry;
And with Snip, snap, the Poets meaning worry,
Like Bullies hide your wants in bounce & Vapour,
If Mem'ry fail—take Snuff, laugh, Curse, & Caper;
Hey Jack! what! — damn it! ha! ha! Cloud, dull, sad,

Cuss it! Hell Devil! Woman, Wine, drunk, Mad!
Now get into the road as fast as you can, & drive away—

Life's a Postchaise, oil it with pleasure Boy,
Smooth run the Wheels, when they are greas'd with Joy!   [*Capers*]

You should always Caper off here——
Smooth run the Wheels etc

WESTON: With all my heart.
Life's a Postchaise etc

[*They all caper off repeating the Lines, & he on the other side.*]

BAYES: Very well on all sides—Let me see an Audience that won't be mov'd with that.

[*he turns & seeing them gone stares & drops his Voice.*]
They are mov'd indeed!—where the Devil are they?

[*he turns to the other side*]

Now M^r. Weston mind & Caper in again repeating
    Life's a Postchaise etc.

WESTON [*without*]: I'll Caper no more——

BAYES [*approaching the side Scene*]: What do you say?

WESTON [*Entring*]: I'll Caper no more I tell you.

BAYES: You won't Caper any more!—but I'll make you
Caper, & to some tune—where's the manager?

WESTON: You had better keep your passion for your next
Tragedy, it is thrown away upon me—I'll Caper no more
I tell you.

BAYES: I'll appeal to the Town & make you caper.

WESTON: So will I, & make you both Curse & Caper.

BAYES: You don't know what I have to say to them.

WESTON: I can say Something to 'Em too.

BAYES: That you may not run your head against a Wall,
(which perhaps would not hurt you) I will tell you what
I'll Say to them.

WESTON: Come along I'll answer it.

BAYES [*addressing himself to the House*]: Ladies & Gentlemen (I wish from my heart there was Somebody in the
House to hear me) Ladies & Gentlemen——

WESTON: So far I am with you—*Ladies & Gentlemen*

BAYES: Here's a very Silly fellow of an actor

WESTON: Of an Author I say——

BAYES: Who can scarce read

WESTON: Who cant write——

[143]

BAYES: and knows nothing of his Profession

WESTON: No—nothing of his Profession.

BAYES: If you will Suffer such a Pigmy insignificant Fellow to laugh at me—& not take it ill

WESTON: I am often laugh'd at, & never take it ill——

BAYES: I say Gentlemen & Ladies if you will not drive such a little Blockhead from the Stage, you will not have a single Author of Merit to write for you.

WESTON: And I say Gentlemen & Ladies, if you will not drive such a great Blockhead from the Stage,—You will not have a Single Author of Merit, to write for you.—If Nature is to be turn'd out of doors, there will be nothing but ranting & roaring in Tragedy & Capering & face making in Comedy—the Stage will go to Ruin, the Publick will go to Sleep, & I shall go to Jail, & there will be an end of poor Johnny Pringle & his Pig. [*Exit*]

BAYES: Johnny Pringle &—what am I reduc'd to!—Very fine, very fine! & so here I am left to cool my heels by myself again! This is a settled & determin'd Plan to affront me! I will keep down my Bile if possible.

[*whistles & walks about*]

It won't do — The Devil has got the better, & I must leave my Curses behind me—may this House be always as Empty as it is now; or if it must fill, Let it be with fine Ladies to disturb the actors, fine Gentlemen to admire themselves, & fat Citizens to Snore in the Boxes;—may the Pit be fill'd with Nothing but Crabbed Cricks, unemploy'd Actors, & Managers Orders—May places be kept in the Green Boxes without being paid for; & may the Galleries

never bring good humour & horse laughs with them again.
—If ever I honour this place with my Wit & presence
again, may I for my folly be doom'd to be an Actor here in
the Winter, & get Money by Tumbling & Rope Dancing in
the Summer. Now my Minds easy — [*Sighs*] Sic transit
Gloria Mundi.   [*Exit*]

Finis

NOTES

THE MEETING OF THE COMPANY

TITLE PAGE: Kemble's note—Collated & Perfect. J.P.K. 1800.

PAGE 125. *Mr. Hopkins:* the prompter of Drury Lane Theatre.

PAGE 125. *Coronations, Installations, etc.*: These have reference to the various spectacular performances given at the Drury Lane Theatre, which kept the carpenter and scene-painter extremely busy. The Coronation of George III and Queen Charlotte (1761) was celebrated at both Drury Lane and Covent Garden with a pageant on the stage. On this occasion, Garrick was outdone by his rival manager at Covent Garden. *The Institution of the Order of the Garter* was presented at Drury Lane October 28, 1771, in celebration of the installation of the Knights of the Garter at Windsor Castle.

PAGE 125. *Master's head.* Garrick's.

PAGE 126. *Parsons.* William Parsons made his first appearance on the stage at Edinburgh in 1759. There he achieved great success in the characters of old men. Engaged by Garrick, by whom he was instructed and encouraged, he soon acquired high rank in the theatre as a low comedian. He possessed excellent humor and had a perfect knowledge of the stage. His forte lay in characterizations of old men.

PAGE 126. *The Country:* The provinces.

PAGE 126. *Miss Platt:* She was one of the minor actresses of Garrick's company.

PAGE 129. *Tom Weston* (1737–1776) was the son of the first cook to King George II. At sixteen he became

much attached to the stage. He finally procured an engagement at Foote's Theatre in the Haymarket where, after
achieving great success in his performance of Jerry Sneak
in Foote's *The Mayor of Garrat*, he was engaged by Garrick. He was one of the finest comedians on the English
stage. His various characterizations caused the theatre to
ring with laughter while he himself did not move a muscle
of his face. Garrick had all he could do to keep countenance
when playing Archer (*Beaux Stratagem*) to Weston's
Scrub. Weston's by-play was excellent. He earned considerable salaries, but was always in debt. He died of
habitual drunkenness.

PAGE 131. *Jerry Sneak*—in Foote's *Mayor of Garrat*.
This was one of Weston's best parts.

PAGE 131. *Dr. Last*—in Foote's *The Devil Upon Two
Sticks*. This too was one of Weston's excellent characterizations.

PAGE 131. *Tragedian*. This was the type of actor Garrick disliked greatly.

PAGE 132. *Hurst*. He was part of the Drury Lane forces
for several years but played mostly in the provinces, in
Dublin particularly. His abilities were even below medi-
ocrity. He played such parts as Polixenes in *Florizel and
Perdita*, Garrick's version of *The Winter's Tale*, and Ven-
tidius in Dryden's *All for Love*.

PAGE 133. *Bransby* was a performer of some merit. His
Kent in *Lear* and his characterization of Downright (*Every
Man in his Humour*) were particularly good.

PAGE 134. *Baddeley*. In the early years of his life,

Robert Baddeley visited the Continent and acquired some knowledge of French. Coming to Drury Lane as an actor, he won considerable applause in low comedy parts, particularly footmen. Frenchmen were his forte. He was an excellent Canton (the French valet) in Garrick and Colman's comedy, *The Clandestine Marriage*.

PAGE 135. *Thomas King* (1730–1805). He was an actor in the very first rank of the profession. The ease of his manner, his splendid voice, and fine form won for him the great success which he enjoyed throughout his career. He excelled particularly as the speaker of a prologue or epilogue, and made certain prologues so extremely popular that the audience would not permit the performance to begin unless King gave the called-for prologue. He achieved great success in the part of Lord Ogleby in *The Clandestine Marriage*, but he reached the climax of his career when he created the part of Sir Peter Teazle in the *School for Scandal*.

PAGE 137. *First little Man:* Garrick.

PAGE 144. Garrick voicing his opinion concerning playwrights and actors.

PAGE 144. Garrick's censure of his audience.

[151]